BLACK
CIVIL WAR VETERANS
IN WASHINGTON STATE

Cynthia A. Wilson

FOREWORD BY
DENISE R. OTTOSON, WASHINGTON STATE CIVIL WAR HISTORIAN

THE
History
PRESS

Published by The History Press
Charleston, SC
www.historypress.com

First published 2024

Manufactured in the United States

ISBN 9781467156134

Library of Congress Control Number: 2023946685

Notice: The information in this book is true and complete to the best of our knowledge. It is offered without guarantee on the part of the author or The History Press. The author and The History Press disclaim all liability in connection with the use of this book.

CONTENTS

FOREWORD

My first glimpse of Cynthia Wilson came sometime in the early 2000s, during a brief encounter with two women on the small grounds of the Grand Army of the Republic Cemetery on Capitol Hill, Seattle. Cynthia Wilson and Jacqueline Lawson told me that they were looking for Black soldiers. I knew that three of them were indeed buried in the GAR Cemetery. I had already been doing research on the residents of the cemetery (the first leg of twenty years of attempting to find every Civil War veteran in the state of Washington). I gushed about the unusual headstone of Gideon "Stump" Bailey, wished them well and went about whatever I was there for.

Even twenty years ago, online genealogical research was in its infancy. Research meant developing arthritis in your wrist scrolling through microfilm and microfiche in the archives of the local branch of the National Archives or the newspaper files of the Seattle Public Library or the university libraries. Rare typewritten manuscripts of previous research sometimes showed up in the unlikeliest of places, often in the files of personal collectors. The wealth of online databases now in existence were a pipe dream.

Researchers with similar interests found ways to talk to one another, while recognizing our differences in focus and scope. We happily shared our hard-found information, while giving each other credit. Cynthia and I began trading information via e-mail. Once sharing started, it continued until the end of 2021, when I put copies of my databases in local, state and Sons of Union Civil War Veterans (SUCWV) archives and ended my work. Her choice of researching a small subset of the thousands of Civil

War veterans in the state meant that she could spend the time and energy necessary for far deeper biographies of the men than I could, given the huge four-generational database I was developing.

Cynthia's work is unique in focusing on the veterans themselves. She does so with an appreciation of their humanity—good, bad or complicated. Back when I started researching the GAR Cemetery residents, a woman with the neighborhood group Friends of the GAR, which kept an eye on the grounds, requested that I tell "who these people were." Whether Cynthia Wilson heard that same request or not, that is exactly, with exceptional dedication, what she has done for these three dozen veterans.

DENISE R. OTTOSON,
Historian, Washington State Civil War Soldiers,
and recipient of the Long Term Project Award from
Association of King County Historical Organizations (AKCHO)

ACKNOWLEDGEMENT OF
APPRECIATION

My sincerest thanks go out to Samuel Mack of U.S. Senator Maria Cantwell's Washington office. I asked for his help in getting a copy of Jasper Evans's and Rudolph Scott's pension files. It had taken me almost two years to get a copy of the files. Sam was very diligent in getting to the right governmental agencies and officials. Thanks, Sam.

Much thanks to Marilyn Quincy for spending time with me discussing her Civil War ancestor William P. Stewart, his family's history and for sharing his photo album with me.

I am forever grateful to Donna Kennedy for sharing family photos of her great-grandfather's family. We must have shared hundreds of e-mails about Clark Harris, and we shared a byline in the *Issaquah Press* dated February 25, 2009. I was able to find for Donna a much-wanted picture of the family home in Issaquah.

Thanks to Lakesha Kimbrough for giving me her connection to two of these brave men.

I would like to thank Denise Ottoson for passing along several soldiers she found in her research of Washington State Civil War soldiers.

Thank you, Loretta-Marie Dimond, for doing a good job of editing this manuscript. I also want to thank your husband, Jim, for that little push about Henry Carper.

Thanks to staff at the National Archives and Records Administration (NARA), Seattle, Washington.

Lastly, many thanks to my very best friend, Jacqueline E.A. Lawson, for the years of encouragement, her expert genealogical assistance and her many trips to NARA when I could not go. She has a family connection to Gilford Hervey—their slave families share common family owners. She passed away before I could finish.

INTRODUCTION

With the issuance of the Preliminary Emancipation Proclamation in September 1862, African Americans—both free and runaway slaves—came forward to volunteer for the Union cause in substantial numbers. Beginning in October, approximately 180,000 African Americans, including 163 units, served in the U.S. Army, and 18,000 in the U.S. Navy. African Americans constituted 10 percent of the entire Union army by the end of the war, and nearly 40,000 died over the course of the war.[1]

General Orders No. 143, issued by the War Department's Adjutant General's Office on May 22, 1863, established the Bureau of Colored Troops:

> *A bureau is established in the Adjutant General's Office for the record of all matters relating to the organization of Colored Troops. An office will be assigned to the chart of the Bureau, with such number of clerks as may be designated by the Adjutant General.*

Thus began the authorized enlistment of free men of color, slaves and contrabands into the Union army.

This book is about my quest to identify African American Civil War soldiers who, for whatever reason, found their way to the Washington Territory/ state. What you will find here is their military history taken from already published sources, and I have supplemented their regimental and company histories with information from muster roll cards and staff field reports (National Archives and Records Administration Record Series M594) and

28th United States Colored Infantry. *Courtesy of Library of Congress.*

their compiled service records. Their pension records are full of information about their quest for monies to help them survive the physical and mental effects of the Civil War and the ultimate complications associated with aging.

I started searching for these brave men with the intention of only finding those buried in Seattle who had a matching Civil War pension file. I soon learned that Washington State had many old soldiers with stories of their own to tell. I expanded my search to cover the entire state—like eating the entire elephant in one sitting. It has taken me nearly twenty years to find thirty-three men through established genealogical research techniques and help from my best friend, Jacqueline E.A. Lawson. I am sure there are others, but I only concentrated on those Black men whose pension records were available.

Their pension files told a rich history of their families with names, dates and stories of injuries incurred during the civil conflict and the suffering from common diseases that they mostly did not recover from as they aged.

For many of these men, it took years to obtain their pension money because of standards set by the pension board.

For others, the pension money was not forthcoming. For most African Americans, it became a very difficult journey. These men and their eventual widows were required to produce documents that most African Americans at the time did not have, such as birth, marriage and death certificates; divorce decrees; and proof of prior marriages.[2] In addition, they needed to provide witnesses to confirm their statements of long-term health issues and most aspects of their life. In many cases, time and distance were factors in obtaining statements. These men were also required to undergo medical examinations by at least three physicians. Many of these men suffered from exposure to intolerable living conditions: "The pension office had a select board of examining surgeons for each county. Some veterans were required to be examined annually or biennially by this board."[3]

As a researcher of family histories, I did not neglect theirs. In a few cases, I contacted living descendants. With their permission I have included their photos (and other photos that I found), and they have enriched this writing with their own family's oral history.

Within this set of men are three Union sailors, two men who worked for the Confederacy, twenty-six Union army soldiers (infantry and light and heavy artillery) and two cooks in all-white regiments; others were free men of color coming from cities as far away as New York; Philadelphia; Boston; New Haven; Jacksonville, Florida; and St. Kitts in the British West Indies. After their service, they traveled long distances and held many occupations before ending their journey in Washington State. They mostly arrived in the late 1880s and early 1900s. A few came when a call went out for miners—not realizing that there was a miner's strike—so they walked into a hornet's nest of unrest; some stayed despite the danger.

To find these men, I used many sources: the 1890 veterans schedule; the 1910 and 1930 censuses, in which soldiers identified military service; local county and city histories; a TV program of a local professor of African American history; another researcher of Civil War soldiers; and my own discoveries while walking cemeteries. I spent many hours going through Ancestry.com looking for soldiers.

Ancestry.com allowed me to use several parameters to flesh out potential soldiers. I scanned censuses for years of birth covering 1830 to 1850, and then I broadened the search to include years of birth prior to 1830. In one instance, I found a soldier born in 1817 who was clearly marked "Colored" on the 1890 veterans schedule for Walla Walla, Washington. On one occasion, a Civil War historian told me of one, but at first blush, I dismissed him because the soldier presented himself as a white man in the 1900s. Getting some pushback from the historian, I took another, closer look. Indeed, the soldier was listed as a "colored man" from his service in the Civil War to the last time he was in Pennsylvania. From the time he left Pennsylvania until he reached Seattle, his race changed from "colored man" to a white citizen in Washington State. In addition, Ancestry and Fold3 had "Compiled Military Service Records" for regiments of the United States Colored Troops. These records had some very unusual documents, including applications for compensation of slaves with their owners identified.

Several of these men were acquainted with one another, and some of these men were even in the same regiments. In my research, I found two soldiers who were cooks in all-white regiments. General Order 323 allowed them to join their respective regiments.

With some difficulty, I obtained the pension file of Jasper Evans Jones, aka Jasper P. Evans, and Rudolph Scott after two years of diligent letter writing and getting assistance from a governmental staffer.

Throughout this entire process, I hoped to be in contact with living descendants of the brave men. I contacted the great-grandchildren of Clark Harris, William P. Stewart, Jessee Donaldson, Jasper Evans and Alfred Samuels; reached out to a woman who was the great-grandniece of Charles James's son, Frederick; located a researcher working for the great-great-grandnephew of Henry Carper; and attempted to contact the spouse of Walter Scott's grandson. I talked with the great-grandniece of Daniel K. Oliver, who was identified as an African American Civil War soldier and a pioneer of a local community. In further research into Oliver's history, I found that Oliver was not an African American but rather was a white Civil War soldier. His ethnicity was misidentified in several publications because of an error made by a researcher.

The research on Henry Carper had initially been completed without the use of his pension file. I sent a request for his pension file in the hopes that the situation with COVID-19 had eased up and that employees at the National Archives and Records Administration (NARA) could go back to work.[4]

I connected with a Steve Cullen of Washington State who was researching Carper for Mr. MacQuarrie, a direct descendant of Henry's, who also lives in Washington State. Between lots of electronic communication with Mr. Cullen, we were able to fill in the details of Henry's life, his mother, his two wives and the possibility of finding the slave owner of Henry and his mother and Henry's stepfather in 1860.

Two sailors, Richard Hazelwood (USS *Volunteer*) and David Franklin (USS *Dawn*), were not included due to time constraints.

PART I

EASTERN WASHINGTON

KITTITAS COUNTY

JESSEE DONALDSON

January 25, 1845–November 19, 1913
Meridianville, Madison County, Alabama—Roslyn, Kittitas County, Washington
Mount Olivet, Roslyn Cemetery
Roslyn, Kittitas County, Washington
Private, Company I, 15th Regiment United States Colored Infantry
January 24, 1863–April 7, 1866
Shelby, Tennessee—Nashville, Tennessee

Jessee was born into slavery and owned by Levi Donaldson of Madison County, Alabama. Jessee said, "I think he was the only owner I ever had."[5] His parents and siblings were unknown until I discovered a family history, *The Donaldson Odyssey: Footsteps to Freedom*, by Lillian Warren Williams; it described a family consisting of Sarah, mother; siblings Cynthia, Susan and Washington; and his wife, Eliza. Jessee's father may have been Levi Donaldson, his owner. Levi's wife, Charlette Amomet, inherited these individuals after the death of Levi's father-in-law, John Amonet of Madison County, Alabama. John's will and his inventory listed the value of Sarah, Cynthia and Susan at $700.[6]

> *Sarah…had given birth to a son, the father was not known but, he was probably a slave of the main house since she had no contact with the field*

slaves. She named her son Washington and was allowed to keep him with her. Two years after the birth of Washington, a son…Sarah named… Jessee Donaldson was born.[7]

Jessee entered the Union army in 1863 in Shelby, Tennessee. His military records tell a different year. Four male Donaldsons were in the same company as Jessee, and all mustered in February 1864.[8]

His time in the army was not without strife. He suffered an injury in an incident in 1864 and was punished by the commanding officer:

I was placed on Picket on a dark night with instructions to not let any body pass without the counter sign (they were expecting an attack…that night) and I heard something approaching with a chain which made a slight giggling and when order to halt it did not but continued to come nearer after calling halt three times, I fired toward the noise and next morning two horses were found dead with a chain around their necks whereupon the Officer of the day order me to be swong up by the thumbs for half a day with my toes bearly touching the ground and I attribute this injury to my left arm and shoulder. The officer of the day was Capt Armstrong of Co. A, 15th regiment U.S.C. I. The guards were on duty about 4 miles from the camp of the Regmt guarding a bridge and the horses were shot approaching the bridge and my post was between the horses and the bridge.[9]

He suffered other injuries, including an injury to his right eye by a piece of a cap blowing into his eye while under orders and in the line of duty. His company had been using blank cartridges on a skirmish drill in Springfield, Tennessee, resulting in photophobia, which worsened as he grew older—he was nearly blind by the end of his life. He also sustained a gunshot wound in the left shoulder in battle during Hood's Raid in 1864.

On October 10, 1865, members of the 15th Regiment were stationed at the Springfield, Tennessee penitentiary, standing guard for the execution of Champ Ferguson, Confederate guerrilla, who was judged guilty in the killing of Union soldiers both Black and white at Saltville, Virginia. There were rumors that the watchers of the hanging were very uncomfortable with "colored" soldiers standing guard.[10]

After his discharge from service, he was employed at Brown's Corral, a government farm in Limestone County, Alabama. In his 1889 disability affidavit, in conjunction with his initial application for a Civil War pension, he stated, "I resided in the following places: near Huntsville Madison County

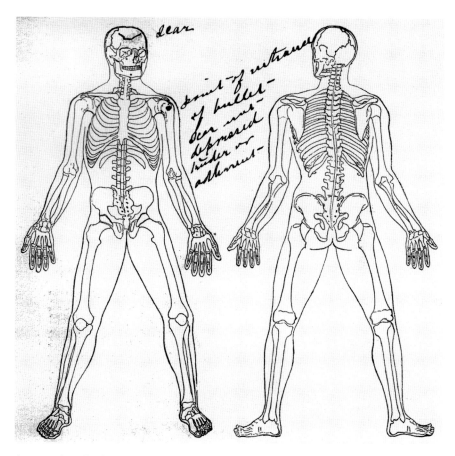

Annotated medical picture from the surgeon's exam. Report in pension file. *Author's collection.*

Ala. I then moved to Pulaski Tenn where my 1st wife died."[11] In a statement taken in June 1901, his son J.J. Donaldson said, "He [Jessee] married, but could not identify his first wife, but that she died in 1869."

For the next twenty-four years, Jessee suffered. In those years, Jessee was examined four times in fifteen years, with different conclusions of the physicians who examined him. Only twice during those examinations did physicians annotate an illustration of a human body. In one illustration was a bullet in the shoulder that was never removed and caused the shoulder and arm to be lame and unusable for any kind of manual labor. A U-shaped scar on his forehead was the result of being kicked by a mule.

Every few years, he was examined by physicians with the same diagnosis: blindness in the right eye, discomfort in the left arm and shoulder and the diminishing capacity to do manual labor to earn a living. But he was not happy with the way he was examined by the physicians:

> *I am the claimant named above whose claim for pension under the act of June 27, 1890, has been rejected on the ground that I am not disabled from manual labor in a pensionable degree and I must say that I am agrieved & surprised at this rejection for I well know that I am and have been long before my Declaration was made—disabled in a pensionable degree.*[12]

Later in the same affidavit, Jessee demanded a physical examination by a doctor of his own choosing:

> *In order to show that the examining Board is sadly mistaken, I have procured a scientific examination and affidavit from Wm. L. Nolen MD who is a reputable Physician of Chattanooga and I respectfully request your honorable department to grant me a new examination….I am confident that when you see the affidavit of Dr Nolen that my case will be reopened.*[13]

Jessee was granted another physical examination administered by Dr. Nolen. In his examination, the doctor found another potential disability that was not recognized in previous physical examinations: a heart condition. He also noticed swelling in the face associated with a "failing heart." Dr. Nolen suggested that Jessee was in no condition to do manual labor and should be granted a pension.

Jessee condemned the government physicians in the way they examined him: they "did not examine me except looking at me and raising my hand up & down." The cost of the examination was paid for by Jessee: $5.25 to Dr. Nolen and $1.00 to Dr. French Harrison. After the completion of the examination, Jessee said:

> *I do believe that great injustice has been done me in this rejecting my claim under the Act of June 27, 1899 and I believe that I should be considered a one armed man as far as "manual labor" and a one eyed man as to vision.*[14]

Jessee was finally approved for six dollars on November 18, 1902. Most if not all these soldiers struggled for years to get a pension that was similarly small, and it would take many years to get more money. All these soldiers would gradually get larger amounts of money until age seventy-two, when they applied for increases.

Jessee resided in Pulaski and Giles Counties, Tennessee, for the next eighteen years and worked in the coal mines. In those eighteen years, he married for a second time to Anna Smalley of Alabama on August 1, 1875. There was no record of their marriage either in Alabama or Tennessee. Four children were born to Jessee and Anna in the first ten years of their marriage in Tennessee: Hattie (1876), General (1878), Thad (1881) and Mary (1883).

While he was living in Tennessee, he ran afoul of the law. He was in court starting on August 20, 1870, for stealing two hogs. Jessee had his day in court in May 1872. He had been sitting in jail for almost two years waiting for trial. Each time he was brought before the judge, the case would be held over for the next court, which resulted in Jessee staying in jail for those two years. The presiding judge, Thomas M. Jones, found Jessee guilty and sentenced him to three years and six months in the state penitentiary. Jessee requested a new trial.

After the birth of Mary, the Donaldson family moved to Trenton, Georgia, where three more children were born: Lizzie (1888), George (1890) and William (1891). With his injuries starting to worsen, Jessee worked as a farmer and a coal miner when he could.

Washington coal mine companies were experiencing serious problems with the coal miners and their strikes. The Donaldsons moved to Washington, where Jessee and three of his sons obtained work as coal miner strikebreakers. Big Jim Shepperson "had been instrumental in bringing some 800 colored miners to Roslyn."[15] Those colored miners broke the strike at Roslyn.

He worked the coal mines until he could no longer work. He and Anna welcomed their last child, Rusia (1897), but little Rusia passed away the next year.

Again Jessee found trouble with the local law enforcement. On December 17, 1902, Jessee was arrested for "selling alcohol to Indian Clarence Johnson on November 3, 1902, in the city of Yakima, Washington." It was a federal crime in the state of Washington to sell alcohol to an Indian under the care of an Indian agent. On December 5, 1902, the *Republican* newspaper reported, "Uncle Sam got after J. Donaldson with a sharp stick." The judge sentenced him to three months at McNeil Island Penitentiary near Steilacoom, Washington, and fined him $50.00. In addition, he was held responsible for the following expenses: clerk's fee, $6.90; marshal's fee, $35.46; and attorney's fee, $10.00, for a total of $52.36 in fees.[16]

With all the trouble the family were dealing with, the illness of Anna added to the pressures. The *Seattle Republican*'s April 1, 1904 edition reported, "Rev. J.P. Brown of Roslyn was in the city [Everett]…whither he went to

Intake photo dated 1921, McNeil Island Penitentiary. *Provided by Pacific Region, NARA, Seattle, Washington.*

be with the family of Mr. Donaldson on account of the very serious illness of Mrs. Donaldson." Jessee lost his Anna on June 9, 1904, in the city of Everett, Washington, with interment taking place at Evergreen Cemetery in the same city. Life became even more difficult for Jessee and family.

By July 26, 1913, "because of inability to support himself on account of ill health and age," he applied for admittance into the Soldiers Home at Orting, Washington. He was approved on July 26, 1913, and entered the home on August 2, 1913. He died on November 19, 1913, at his own home.[17] Jessee was buried in the colored section of Mount Olivet Cemetery in Roslyn, Washington. Son Thad and daughter Rusia are also buried at Mount Olivet.

Jessee left many descendants. I contacted one such descendant, LaKeshia. She is the third-great-granddaughter of Jessee Donaldson and resides in Seattle. She is also the third-great-granddaughter of Alfred Samuels, another Civil War soldier. Recently I was introduced to Jessee's fourth-great-grandson Ray and Jessee's fifth-great-grandson Ryan at a meeting of the Black Genealogy Research Group of Seattle. We have exchanged lots of information both known and unknown to us. The family now has a picture of the patriarch Jessee Donaldson. They were thrilled to have his image.

My research has only been about Jessee and his early life. Descendants of Jessee have published his entire story under the title "The Donaldsons Stand Amongst Roslyn's Black Pioneers" by Alisa Weis and Ryan Anthony Donaldson.

FRANCIS (FRANK) M. HENSON

November 2, 1843–January 9, 1917
Shelbyville, Shelby County, Illinois—Ellensburg, Kittitas County, Washington
Independent Order of Odd Fellows Cemetery
Ellensburg, Kittitas County, Washington
Private, Company C, 29ᵗʰ Regiment United States Colored Infantry
November 3, 1864–November 6, 1865
Jacksonville, Illinois—Brownsville, Texas

This soldier was born a free person of color. It's unclear how his parents moved to Illinois from Missouri (birthplace of his mother) or Virginia (birthplace of his father). It is assumed that his parents were slaves at some point in their history. No siblings have been identified.

At the start of the war, Frank was hired as a paid (by the government) servant to Colonel Gustavus A. Smith. The colonel became the commanding officer of the 35ᵗʰ Illinois Volunteer Infantry from 1861 through 1864. Frank's length of service with the 35ᵗʰ was the same as the colonel's. Early during the war, Smith was wounded badly and removed from field duty to recuperate from his injuries.

Frank enlisted in the U.S. Colored Troops in 1864. Originally assigned to Company A of the 29ᵗʰ, he was later transferred to Company C. He enlisted in the city of Jacksonville, Illinois, and transferred to Camp Butler on December 29, 1864. The muster and descriptive roll showed that Frank had enlisted for one year. He was nineteen, had black eyes and hair, was of Black complexion and was five feet, four inches tall.

After the surrender of Lee's army to Grant, this regiment's assignment before mustering out was at Ringgold Barracks in Texas. Company C boarded the *William Kennedy* steamer transport on June 9, 1865, to arrive at Mobile by June 10, 1865, to travel to Brazos, Santiago, but rough seas

Military headstone. *Findagrave.com.*

prevented the landing and forced the transport to land in Galveston. Weather permitted the *Kennedy* to land at Brazos on June 24.

For the next several months, this company remained in Texas, stationed in several cities, including White's Ranch and Ringgold, before arriving at Brownsville, Texas, and mustering out.

After the end of the war, Frank returned to Illinois and maintained his residence in Springfield. Between 1873 and 1888, he was in trouble with the law. His antics were regularly reported in several Springfield newspapers.

A lover he was not. In January 1873, he was charged with brutally beating his "sweetheart," Ann Beasley, after which he was released after paying a fine of ten dollars and court costs. As a point of repudiation, he had a warrant sworn out for Ann for "language and conduct calculated to provoke a breach of peace." She paid a fine of three dollars and costs.[18] The following month, on February 5, he married Miss Beasley.[19]

He had a difference of opinion with two men that was especially brutal. Tom Mills and Albert Murrell both could have lost their lives. Henson's weapons of choice were "a razor and a knife." In July 1879, Mills was assaulted by Henson with a razor, "cut[ting]…the right shoulder blade about six inches in length and another on the arm from the shoulder down to the elbow…severing some of the arteries.…A warrant was issued in October 1888 for Henson for intent to kill Albert Murrell in a row in Birdsong's saloon" on a Friday night. In none of the court cases did Henson accrue any jail time, but rather he was fined and paid court costs. The October 4, 1888 *Daily Illinois State Journal*'s headline called him the "Notorious Frank Henson."

The next year, the Springfield newspaper reported that he boarded the Chicago & Alton Railway in Springfield on Monday, January 28, 1889, bound for Ellensburg, to meet up with his good friend John B. Fogarty in the city.

A write-up suggested that Henson was the first African American in Ellensburg, Washington, arriving there in 1886. Frank did not arrive in Ellensburg until 1889, according to the local newspaper of Springfield, Illinois. Even his obituary stated that he arrived in Ellensburg in 1888. So, there are three different years that Henson arrived in Ellensburg. Which is correct? Was he really the first African American in Ellensburg? An obituary for Alfred Paradise suggested that he was in the county in 1887.[20] The armed convoy of strikebreakers and guards arrived in Roslyn on August 21, 1888.

He became an upstanding citizen of that city, working with horses on the Fogarty Ranch and the Washington Dairy Creme company as a driver. The local obituary stated, "He has always been a good citizen…. He was an amiable, honest man and had the respect of all who knew him."[21] The members of the town probably didn't know about his life in Springfield, Illinois.

By age seventy-three, Henson's health was slowly going downhill. He was soon assisted by attorney Edward Pruyn, who "agrees to take said sum [ten dollars] in full compensation for his services."[22] His declaration of invalid pension was drawn up and witnessed by J.B. Fogarty and William Freyburger. His application to the pension board was approved. In a deposition given by Henson on August 12, 1904, in his appearance before the clerk of the Superior Court of Kittitas County of Washington State, he stated that he was "in part incapacitated from earning support by his manual labor by reason of his age, and by having both arms broken and breastbone broken from the kick of a horse about three years ago."

In an examination of Frank, the doctor noted the reasons for approving the pension for Frank:

> *I find no evidence of vicious or depraved habits. Applicant is in my judgement entitled to disability rating of 6/18 for senility and 3/18 for heart trouble and 2/18 for trouble of the left shoulder and arm.*[23]

Those disabilities were the reason he was given his initial pension of six dollars.

Henson lived in Ellensburg until his death in January 1917. At the time of his death, he left no will. George Davis petitioned the court to become the administrator of Henson's estate. His assets included a small house and small portion of a lot. George was accepted as the administrator on March 30, 1917, and immediately petitioned the court to proceed with the private sale of the only asset, the house. The notice of the sale was posted. At first, one individual responded. George Janks offered $202.50. It was revealed later that another offer had been submitted by R.O. Broust in the amount of $250, or $25 above the assessed value of $225. The court denied Janks's offer and accepted the Broust offer. The house's location was described as "Lot 9 and factional lot 10, block 66, Murray's addition to Ellensburg, land is S1/2 of SE 1/4 of section 11, Township 16, Range 17, EWM, Kittitas County Washington."[24]

He left no descendants in Washington State. There is the possibility that he had a child, R.H. Henson, by Ann Beasley Henson. A Springfield, Illinois newspaper dated 1916 reported that R.H. Henson was visiting his father, Frank Henson.[25]

SPOKANE COUNTY

ALONZO STEVEN ADKINS

1837–August 8, 1897
Manhattan, Kings County, New York—Spokane, Spokane County, Washington
Greenwood Memorial Terrace
Spokane, Spokane County, Washington
Private, Company D, 11th Regiment, United States Colored Heavy Artillery (formerly
14th Rhode Island Colored Heavy Artillery)
Providence, Rhode Island–New Orleans, Louisiana
September 10, 1863—October 2, 1865

The information on this soldier was sparse. He applied for his pension in July 1897 and died the following month. When his pension file was received, it consisted of six pages.

Alonzo was born a free man of color in Kings County, New York, to Thomas F. and Mary Henry Adkins. His siblings consisted of brothers Theodore, Alfred and John and sisters Charlotte and Mary. He married Lenora Williams on June 5, 1874, in Manhattan, New York. There were no apparent children born to this union.

Several General Orders were issued to establish the Rhode Island Colored Artillery. General Order 36 established the colored regiments, Order 24 established a training facility and Order 30 established the first four companies.

After completing training at Dexter Training Ground in Providence, Alonzo's regiment sailed on the steamer *City of Newport* for Newport on December 19, 1863, and then boarded the transport *Catawba*. They arrived in New Orleans on December 30 and remained in New Orleans until January 3, 1864.

On January 3, the 1st Battalion boarded the transport and proceeded to Passo Cavallo, Texas, and occupied Fort Esperanza on Matagorda Island. The fort underwent repairs by the Union forces, who used it as their base of operations for further campaigns in the area. In the spring of 1864, the Union troops withdrew from Matagorda Bay to participate in the invasion of Texas from northeast Louisiana. After the last of the federals left Matagorda Island on June 15, Fort Esperanza was reoccupied by the Confederates and held until the end of the war.[26]

It was at Fort Esperanza that Companies A, C and D, in a protest of pay inequity, refused to accept their pay and were arrested for insubordination. These men were angry about the pay system—free Black soldiers were receiving ten dollars versus white soldiers receiving twelve dollars per month. This changed on June 15, 1864. On the other hand, Black soldiers who were slaves when they enlisted did not receive the same pay as their free Black brothers until March 3, 1865.[27] The court transferred the guilty ringleaders to Fort Jefferson, Florida.

The only action seen by this company was at Indian Village, Louisiana, on August 6, 1864. Major Richard Shaw reported:

> [H]*is pickets were attacked this morning by about one hundred mounted infantry. They drove in the pickets at first, and about fifty of them got into town. They then retreated toward the* [Indian] *village, carrying their wounded in a wagon. Our loss is three killed and wounded, and four taken prisoners; their loss is supposed to be about the same.*[28] [The casualties from Company G included Samuel O. Jefferson, Anthony King and Samuel Mason. Major Shaw reported that those men were] *taken from our pickets the other day and were shot by their captors after crossing the bayou at Indian Village….They were foully murdered.*[29]

Alonzo's company returned to New Orleans via the steamer *Clinton*; they reached New Orleans on May 23, 1864. The regiment mustered out in the city. Five days later, the 1st Battalion boarded the steamship *North Star* for the voyage north to New York. A passenger described the voyage as "stormy and tempestuous." The steamer arrived in New York on October 15, 1865, and was quarantined for twenty-four hours.

"In the afternoon of the following day (the 17th) the regiment made a street parade, which was seen by crowds of people, with hearty demonstrations of applause. The New York papers made favorable comments on the fine appearance of the command as it marched through the streets."[30]

The *New York Daily Reformer* dated October 19, 1865, described the return of the 11th Colored Regiment.

A New York telegram printed in the same paper noted:

> *A no more imposing spectacle has been presented to the citizens of New York since the commencement of the return of our soldiers than was witnessed this afternoon in the march of the 11th U.S. Colored Heavy Artillery, Col. Sypher, up Broadway, preceded by a brass band of some thirty pieces and a drum corps of equal number, all colored.…The soldiers appeared to appreciate the reception which was the warmest that has been extended to any of our returning heroes.*[31]

Alonzo spent his time in the service in military hospitals for health issues, including fevers, bronchitis and diarrhea. His declaration dated July 13, 1897, listed several reasons why he was not able to support himself: liver enlargement, rupture, dropsy, pleurisy, lung trouble and permanent cough. These ailments probably secondarily contributed to his death.

Alonzo was a resident of Spokane, Washington, for at least eight years prior to his death. He spent most of his life in New York City with a short stay in Boston. He worked as a butcher and later a porter. No living descendants of Alonzo were found. His grave is unmarked.

PETER BARNABUS BARROW

1843–July 6, 1906
Virginia—Spokane, Spokane County, Washington
Greenwood Cemetery
Spokane, Spokane County, Washington
Private, Company A, 66th Regiment, United States Colored Infantry
March 11, 1864–March 20, 1865
Vicksburg, Mississippi—Natchez, Mississippi

I was born a slave near Petersburg VA and was taken away from there when quite young down to Alabama when I grow to manhood….My father's name was Thompson, but I don't remember his first name….I was sold to Wm Johnson by speculators and taken to Ala. Mr. Johnson lived in Chambers Co. Ala, at different places. He gave me to his daughter Mary who married Jackson Barrow who lived near Cosita Ala, and he moved onto a place of his own near West Point, Ga., and his place in Ala. I lived with the Jackson Barrow until the Union Army came through there in the spring of 1864, when I with another slave Luke Barrow went to Vicksburg Miss and we both went into the same reg't.[32]

During the service our regiment was divided and set to different points. My Co. left Fort Hill, Vicksburg and went to Goodrick's Ldg (Louisiana) and remained there during the summer of 1864. In the fall the Co. went over into Arkansas to White River at a point called St. Charles. I was not with them there—being in hospital—reg'tal hospital—at Goodrick Ldg. I remained in the reg'tal hospital about two years being sick and nursing the sick.[33]

Peter Barrow resided in Warren County, Mississippi, where he served as an elected official in the state House of Representatives from December 1869 to 1872 and was considered a "Radical Free Negro."[34] In 1874, he was elected to the state senate.

At the end of Reconstruction, living in Mississippi became difficult. For Peter, being a Black legislator was a dangerous occupation.

Peter and his family arrived in Washington State in the fall of 1889. He became politically active. His achievements included the founding of the John Logan Colored Republican Club, his nomination to the Populist Party and leading the Farmer's Alliance Movement in Washington State.

Peter Barrow. *Courtesy of blackpast.org.*

In 1890, he and his wife, along with several others, established the oldest historically Black church in Spokane, where Reverend Barrow served as pastor from 1895 to 1906. In July 1902, he helped host the Third Annual State Convention of the Colored Baptist Church at Calvary, giving an evening address to the attendees.[35]

Peter and his family were well known in the Spokane community. Barrow took advantage of the Homestead Act of 1862[36] and purchased 160 acres;

he purchased an additional 160 acres as a cash sale entry in both Stevens County and Ferry County.[37] The first 160 acres purchased in Stevens County was on the east side of Deer Lake and was developed into a resort. In addition, he started a fruit farm in the same area. According to the *Spokane Press*, Peter stated:

> *I want to tell you that we have started the greatest fruit farm in the world— the greatest because it is the most novel. We have planted 25,000 fruit trees, and every tree is billed to raise red apples. We have the finest fruit producing country in the state and you can imagine how red that country will be painted when those 25,000 trees go on shift.*[38]

With partner Charles Parker, son Charles owned the *Spokane Citizen* for the years between 1908 and 1913 and was the city's first Black newspaper owner. After being a "printer's devil" for the *Spokane Review*, he later opened the X-Ray Printing Company, which was "in a prosperous state and is the most extensive plant of its kind owned by a Negro on the Pacific Coast."[39] His shop was located on Bernard Street in Spokane, and according to the October 3, 1902 edition of the *Seattle Republican*, "This gentleman competes with the largest shops in the city and has all he can attend to." The printing company was in business until his death in 1950.

Peter Barrow lost his life several days after an accident in Tacoma, Washington. Locals described the accident, in which a streetcar carrying thirty persons, including Barrow, hit a metal plate in the street. The streetcar was brought to a sudden stop, throwing its passengers forward. Several of the passengers had minor injuries, including Barrow.

The local medical service transported Barrow to a nearby hospital for examination. The attendant reported that he would be fine and could be released in a few days—that was Monday at 5:45 p.m. The *Seattle Republican* reported that the group had attended a Baptist convention in Tacoma, of which Barrow was a delegate from Spokane, and that the accident occurred while the group was returning from a picnic sponsored by the convention.[40]

The *Tacoma Daily News* reported on July 30, 1906, that an autopsy held by Coroner Stewart, assisted by Dr. E.M. Brown and Dr. Shaver, disclosed a uremic condition that, together with the shock, caused the death. "Thursday, he [Barrow] had a sinking spell, and at his request word was sent for his wife and two children. Saturday his eldest son arrived and was present when his father died."[41] As for the cause of his death, his death certificate does not

Loaded cable car, Court House Hill, Tacoma, Washington, circa 1906. *Courtesy of Library of Congress.*

affirm his death as an accident—hit by streetcar—but rather that he died of uremic poisoning.

One of the consequences of the accident was a lawsuit filed against Tacoma Railway & Power Company by his son, Charles, on behalf of his minor siblings, John and Benjamin. Judge Kennan "said there was doubt if the company was liable for any damages at all."[42] He received $150 nonetheless.

In recalling and relating our oral history, we sometimes misinterpret historical facts and data. With that said, the family passed along their oral history through interviews and through writings of other historians using the same oral history. A story of Peter following General Sherman to the sea was just a myth. Peter spent almost two years hospitalized in Louisiana and later was a nurse in that hospital. Peter recorded this information in documents within his pension file.

The *Spokane Daily Chronicle* dated July 30, 1906, described Peter's "Noble Life":

> *He was for many years very active in religious, charitable and political movements; affecting the welfare of his race....Rev. Barrow was nominated for presidential elector on the populist ticket and ran several thousand votes ahead of his ticket. In 1894, he was nominated for the lower house by the Populist Party, and again ran ahead of his ticket. In the later years he retired from the political activity, devoting himself to charitable and religious work exclusively.*

Peter left descendants in Washington and California, including twin great-grandsons who were professional boxers.

CHARLES WARREN JAMES

November 15, 1824–October 28, 1925
Jay, Essex County, New York—Spokane, Spokane County, Washington
Riverside Memorial Park Cemetery
Spokane, Spokane County, Washington
United States Navy
USS Potomska
December 20, 1861–August 29, 1862

Charles Warren was born to Peter and Eliza James—all were free people of color. His parents were natives of Holland and were the parents of four known children (two girls, Ursula and Rachael, and one other boy, Peter), born in New York.

> *I enlisted in the United States Navy in the city of Boston, Massachusetts, August 1, 1860, on the United States Ship "Relief"...being called on*

board a store ship…my service on board the "Relief" and…"Potomska" was as cook for the officers, called ward-room cook. I continued the "Potomska" in service until August 1862, when, upon her arrival in Philadelphia, I was sent on board the Receiving Ship "Princeton," and discharged…August 29, 1862.[43]

According to James's hospital records, he was treated for hearing loss while the *Potomska* was in Philadelphia for repairs in August 1862. The doctor determined that his deafness was not attributable to his work duty.

After his discharge from the navy, James spent his time wandering between New York and Boston. He worked as a porter for a doctor, Judge B.R. Curtis and New York actress Clara Morris.[44]

Charles married several times and had children by his second and fourth wives. The second wife, Martha Freeman, was the mother of six children, born in Vermont, Connecticut and New York between 1846 and 1857. His fourth wife, Sarah Talbot, was the mother of four. Charles, in his eagerness to marry so many women, forgot to obtain divorces to free himself to

Clara Morris, New York actress. *Courtesy of Library of Congress.*

32

marry the next wife. His marriage to his first wife, Louisa Virginia, was not one that the pension examiners could confirm. His second wife, Martha Freeman, was confirmed by the examiners after years of searching, and Martha's recollection of the date was faulty. She married Charles on March 12, 1846. He married for a third time to Mary E. Leslie on May 26, 1866, in Boston; the examiner could not find any indication that either of them obtained a divorce. Charles's deposition of March 18, 1909, stated that Mary, after being married to him for three years, left him and married another man, which made both marriages illegal. He complicated the situation by living with Martha on and off during the births of their six children—the eldest born in 1846 and the youngest born in 1857. Charles deserted Martha and supplied no financial support from the time of their marriage to her death in 1909. Their daughter Alice James Freeman noted in her deposition of November 12, 1926:

> *At the time he visited Mother here we were living on North Champlain Street—No 54....Father staid about a week, and...I did not see him and mother in bed together....When I said to him that he had done very little for us he replied that he knows it, but that he was foolish when he was young. I know very little of where Father lived after leaving Mother. Letters have come from Boston, Scituate and Spokane.*[45]

Charles's fourth marriage was to Sarah Talbot on April 28, 1878, in Boston. Still, he had not divorced Martha when he married Sarah. This fact would complicate her ability to obtain her widow's pension.

In March 1890, while living in West Scituate, Massachusetts, Charles made application to the pension board for monetary assistance because of health issues. Part of the process included an examination by a medical doctor in April. The doctor found that his health was not as bad has he had stated. It took another seventeen years before he received his first payment of $28.10.

The family remained in Boston until about 1897 before moving to Spokane, Washington. Approaching seventy-three, he could no longer work as a porter due to deafness and rheumatism. He stated that his health issues started while aboard the USS *Potomska*. The ship was stationed off the coasts of South Carolina and Florida. While the ship would travel up small rivers, it would get stuck. "Often the boat would run ashore in the narrow rivers, we would get out and in the wet pull her off. In that way the rheumatism came upon me."

When he applied for his pension, the pension examiners found issues with his application. His wife, Martha, had applied for a widow's pension in 1862 because she was under the impression, from information from her mother-in-law, Eliza James, that Charles had been killed in the Civil War. The pension board investigated the situation, and Martha was told that they could not confirm his death or his military service at the time. It would take some years before the confusion resolved itself. The board informed Martha that her husband had been in the Civil War but was in the navy and was still alive and living with another woman, reportedly his wife. Martha told the board that she had married Charles (aka Charles Bigelow) in 1846 and had six children by him while they were living in Vermont, and she was entitled to half of his pension. Unfortunately, Martha had forgotten that she had signed a legal document that in exchange for the sum of $100:

> [T]hey will never make any further claim of any kind whatsoever upon said a for support otherwise; that on his death they shall neither have nor claim any right or share in his estate, real or personal; that they will, whenever requested by said trustees, execute and deliver all proper instruments and do whatever is proper to release all claims and rights against said Charles and his property and after his decease against his estate or to assign all such claims and right to said trustee. They further agree that they will not make any claim for pension from the United States of America as the wife, widow or children of 2…further agree not in any way to interfere with the claim of said Charles James for a pension…if they violate any of the foregoing agreements they will return to him [trustee] said sum of one hundred dollars.[46]

The pension board disagreed, and she was rejected. The pension examiner also investigated statements made by Martha. They ultimately found that Martha had indeed married Charles on March 12, 1846, in the city of Bristol, Vermont—a marriage certificate was found by the examiner when she could not. Those individuals who knew Martha could not definitely provide proof of her marriage to Charles. By the time the investigation was complete, Martha had died in 1909. Prior to her death, she requested the location of her husband, but that information was not forthcoming from the examiner.

James's fourth wife, Sarah, also applied for a widow's pension. She furnished all the appropriate information requested by the pension examiner. Because of the situation with the second wife, her claim was denied. James was still married to Martha in 1909 when she died. If Sarah had married

James in 1909 after the death of Martha, then she would have been entitled to his pension. Both Martha and Sarah died penniless because of the actions of Charles James.

James left descendants living in Vermont. Sarah's children moved to Oregon and left no living descendants.

CHARLES R. SCOTT (ALIAS RUDOLPH B. SCOTT)

November 12, 1856–1909
New Haven, CT—Spokane, Spokane County, Washington
Fairmont Memorial Park Cemetery
Spokane, Spokane County, Washington
USS Chicopee
May 11, 1964–May 8, 1865

RUDOLPH SCOTT.

Rudolph B. Scott, 1899. *Courtesy of Newspapers.com.*

Rudolph Bowman Scott was born in New Haven, Connecticut, and raised in a family of six children. It is suspected that he used his brother Charles's name at enlistment. Jerri Remsen, a crewmate, gave a notarized statement on March 4, 1880, in Chicago, Illinois, that he knew Rudolph B. Scott to have enlisted under the name of Charles R. Scott. When he joined the Union navy, he was at once assigned to the USS *Carolina* for one day and then transferred to the USS *Chicopee* under the command of A.D. Harrell. He served as a landsman at a salary of twelve dollars per month.

With the invention of the torpedo in early 1863 by John Lay and engineer W.W. Woods and the brashness of a young Lieutenant William B. Cushman, the events of October 27, 1864, introduced this young sailor to war on the water. The historic sinking of the Confederate ram *Albemarle* put Scott in the company of seven future Medal of Honor recipients; he did not obtain the same recognition.[47]

In one exceptionally long statement that Rudolph made, he spoke about his experience of going insane after being hit on the head while handling

35

a torpedo with his mate Jerri Remsen in 1865. It caused a late injury to show up in 1888. He started with relating how he was exposed to malaria at Plymouth, North Carolina, and then entered a facility for the insane:

I was insain part of the first year I came out of the Service and was confined in the Marshal Infirmity of Troy NY and taken from there to the Hartford Insane Retreat at Hartford came at reduced rates on account of Having came out of the service of the country. Since then I have been able to perform manual labor about half of the time & hardly that on the account of my head & wound system caused by the firing of that gun while in the service.[48]

In his pension depositions, he recalled his battlefield encounters:

This injury to head from while I now suffer…was caused by a shock on Thanksgiving Day 1864, while in line of duty, pulling for torpedoes in the Ronoke river, in North Carolina, in a small boat. A masked battery opened on us, when we dropped back to U.S.S Chicopee for orders. Then they fired an eleven inch gun over our heads as we lay alongside the Chicopee.[49]

He stated on December 18, 1896:

A wound on left hand received while dragging for torpedoes in a small boat in river there were two commandos with me at the time one was Edward Houghton who was killed at Norfolk VA and the other one I cannot recall at present. I did not think much of the hurt at the time. Four years later on May 17, 1900, I was one of the men who volunteered on the 27th day of October 1864, or thereabouts, to go with Lieut. Cushman when Lieut. Cushman blew up the Rebel Ram "Albemarle," at Plymouth, N.C., and I, and Jerry Rempson [sic], brought the torpedo up from the hold of the steamer "Chicopee" when the torpedo was placed on the steam launch.[50]

Those Medal of Honor recipients were Lorenzo Denning, Daniel George, Richard Hamilton, Bernard Harley, Edward Houghton, Robert King and Henry Wilkes—all were part of the crew of Picket Boat No. 1. Scott and Remsen were the only two sailors on Picket Boat No. 1 who did not receive the same recognition even though they were participants. A letter to a governmental agency requesting a look at giving Scott the same recognition was denied for lack of confirmation from other sailors.[51]

Rudolph returned to his hometown of New Haven after he was discharged from military service. Before he returned, he spent some time in Chicago working as a mail agent. Rudolph married on December 30, 1869, to Sophia Lowery, in New Haven, and she later died on February 14, 1877, in Penn Yan, New York. Into this family was born Georgia Scott on October 9, 1870, in the city of Rochester, New York. He next married Adele A. Wagoner on September 4, 1883, in Denver, Colorado, and by 1884, the family were living in Spokane, Washington; the couple's first child, Rudolph, was born on June 27, 1884. This couple increased their family with the births of two more children: Henry on May 26, 1886, and Addie on June 30, 1888.

Scott became a community leader almost immediately, as did Adele. Rudolph was very active in the political circles that affected the political fortunes of the Black constituency. Even though the Black population was very small in the city of Spokane during the late 1880s, Rudolph was appointed by the Republican Party as a delegate to the state convention, organizing Washington's government for statehood. He was sent to the state convention hosted in Seattle to choose delegates to the national convention in Minneapolis. It should be noted that this convention also witnessed the appointment of William Lynch as the Speaker's page and the appointment of John Conna as assistant sergeant at arms:[52]

> *In 1895, Scott made his first application for a Civil War pension under the act of June 27, 1890 and the general law. His initial claim for the pension was rejected. Scott appealed to his Congressional Representative Hyde to have him consult with the Pension Board about the rejection. "Representative Hyde has interested himself in this case, because Mr. Scott is greatly disabled, unable to earn the support for his family and in needed circumstances.... The ground for the rejection, however, is that testimony furnished to the department does not show disabilities in a pensionable degree."[53]*

He applied in 1896 and was rejected again "on the ground of no ratable disability shown from alleged injury to head and impaired hearing and malarial poisoning since the date of filing the claim."[54] His application for pension was eventually accepted, as reported in the *Pullman Herald* dated September 25, 1897.

Scott was also actively involved with the Nez Perce tribe and their confrontation with the United States. In 1900, he accompanied Chief Joseph to Washington, D.C., as part of a delegation to present their case. He solicited a favorable opinion for his friend, the great chief.

With the help of General John A. Logan's wife, President Harrison appointed Rudolph to a position in customs. His service was very brief before his removal from that position in 1893. Again, Mrs. Logan stepped in:

> *The Republican noted with much pleasure and satisfaction the appointment of R.B. Scott of Spokane, as Chinese Inspector of the district in and about the city with headquarters in Spokane. Mr. Scott is the first man of his nationality to hold a federal position in the Northwest, having been Deputy Customs Inspector on Osooyos Lake, which position he held with great credit to himself and all convened for four years.*[55]

The *Seattle Republican* of February 16, 1906, reported that "Scott…has been summarily dismissed from duty by Chief Metcalf for official delinquency in his official duties."[56]

"Owing to the fact that Mr. Scott was a Union soldier under the command of General Logan who has taken a special interest in him, and each time has prevailed upon the President to name Mr. Scott to important official positions.…Since that time, Mr. Scott became interested in a mining project that came into his possession and he used to good advantage."[57]

Rudolph Scott's later years would prove creative and productive. He became an accomplished photographer, credited with a famous portrait of his friend Chief Joseph on October 17, 1899, in Spokane. He held offices of various fraternal organizations, including the Masons, the Independent Order of Foresters and the Grand Army of the Republic.

His children Rudolph B. Jr. (1884–1963), Henry W. (1886–1969) and Adaline S. (1888–1921) left no descendants to continue the Scott family name.

WALTER L. SCOTT

October 2, 1847–January 6, 1923
New Richmond, Clermont County, Ohio—Spokane, Washington
Greenwood Cemetery
Spokane, Spokane County, Washington
Company K, 27th Regiment, United States Colored Infantry
August 6, 1864–September 7, 1865
New Richmond, Ohio—New Bern, North Carolina

Walter Scott was born a free person of color in New Richmond, Clermont County, Ohio. His pension file described him as a mulatto, five feet and seven inches tall, with black hair and eyes. His mother, Sophia Hall, may have been a runaway slave and used the Underground Railroad to reach her destination in Ohio. New Richmond was known as one of the cities where the Underground Railroad was most active. It was a thriving community during the antebellum period with a tannery, a distillery and a boat building industry, and its First Presbyterian Church was the center of abolitionism. New Richmond's Black community was the largest in Clermont County. Records indicate a large migration from southern states during this period, including forty-two from Mississippi. This occurred because of strict laws hindering emancipation there. As a result, slaveholders who wished to emancipate their slaves came to Ohio, where the laws made emancipation easier.[58]

As a seventeen-year-old boy, Walter was part of a larger group of boys and men who joined the army from New Richmond—most joined the 27th Regiment of the United States Colored Infantry. This was a big deal for these individuals. By joining in August, Walter missed the horrific Battle of the Crater on July 30, 1864. The regiment was to be among the advance units after the mine explosion, but at the last minute it was placed in reserve. The Black division, including the 5th and 27th USCT, that was to lead the assault was ordered to go around the "Crater," but the white troops who replaced them just before the explosion had no such instructions. The disaster was inevitable. The Black troops sent in at the end of the battle merely made the casualty figures rise.

In December 1864, the 27th was sent north for the assault on Fort Fisher. The fort was called the "Gibraltar of the Confederacy." It guarded the entrance to the port of Wilmington, North Carolina, the largest remaining Confederate port on the Atlantic coast. Several Union attempts to capture the fort earlier in the war had failed miserably. The 1864 effort was to be an all-out assault combining army and navy forces. The 27th was held in reserve until late in the second day of the battle. Union troops had fought hand to hand for every foot of the fort. Finally, on January 13, the Confederates fell back to Battery Buchanan, the citadel of last stand. At 9:30 p.m., the large mass of troops of the 27th was seen in the moonlight from the battery. The order "Forward" was given, and the 27th moved briskly toward the enemy. The struggle was brief but bloody. The last remnant of Fort Fisher was captured, and the surrender of Wilmington soon followed.

The regiment served out the rest of the war as occupation troops in Goldsboro and Wilmington. They were mustered out on September 21,

1865, and most of the men returned to their homes in Brown County, Ohio. The roll of honor shows that the 27th USCT lost 18 killed in action, and 184 died in hospitals from disease or wounds from battle.[59]

OMAHA, NEBRA...

JOSMOPOLITA

HOTEL,

Nos. 37 and 39

MAIN STREE1

Helena, Montana,

CHWAB & ZIMMERMA

PROPRIETORS.

Ad from newspaper for Cosmopolitan Hotel. *From a city directory courtesy of Ancestry.com.*

After the war, Walter returned to New Richmond to start his new life. He took a job as a seafarer on a steamer that probably ran along the Ohio River. In 1868, he married Josephine Hull of Mississippi, and together they had four children: Walter E., Eva M., Minor Larue and Alpha M. This family remained in Ohio until 1880, before moving to Helena, Montana Territory.

For twenty years, this family remained in Helena, where Walter's profession as an "expressman" was the main source of their livelihood. The Cosmopolitan Hotel in Helena employed him from 1881 to 1899.

By 1900, the family were in Spokane, Washington.[60] Josephine died in June, leaving Walter with a family to support. He found jobs as porter in a store; at Bradley Engine & Machine Company; and finally, as a janitor for Fairbanks, Morris & Company. During this time, he suffered with many health issues that eventually compromised his ability to work and provide for his future.

On August 24, 1901, Walter applied for his Civil War pension. His health issues were increasing to the point that manual labor was difficult. He declared what he contracted, when and where: rheumatism in 1867 in Ohio, disease of the kidneys in 1868 in Ohio, piles in 1881 in Montana, disease of the bladder in 1881 in Montana and disease of the lungs since 1866. Like all potential pensioners, he took the required physical examinations. Drs. B.R. Freeman, E.D. Olmster and Geo. W. Libby examined Walter on November 13, 1901, in Spokane. They all agreed:

> We find that the aggregate permanent disability for earning a support by manual labor is due to disease of kidneys (diabetes) not due to vicious habits and warrants a rate of $12.00 per month, claimant unable to do any manual labor.[61]

His application was approved at the warranted rate. Even though he was approved, he continued to work as a porter until his death. He

Military headstone. *Findagrave.com.*

became very active in Grand Lodge Free and Accepted Masons, a fraternal organization in Spokane. This organization on July 20, 1906, was responsible for the placement of the cornerstone at the first building that Mount Zion Baptist Church occupied in Seattle, Washington. Walter's grandson Walter Vernon became grand master for the years 1956 to 1959 while living in Spokane, Washington.

On June 26, 1911, Walter entered a second marriage to the former Alice Maud Highgate Harris of Ontario, Canada. Her first marriage to John T. Harris of Ontario, Canada, ended in a divorce on January 26, 1909, filed by Alice in Spokane, Washington. She remained with Walter until his death in 1923.

After Alice moved to Oakland, California, she applied for a widow's pension on December 28, 1923. She filled out a "Declaration of a Widow for Accrued Pension" and submitted all the required documents as proof of her relationship to Walter. She received five dollars as the accrued balance due to her from Walter's last payment, which would have been fifty dollars if he had survived the month of January. A letter writing campaign to get her widow's pension started on December 1, 1923, running until October 31, 1939:

I cannot understand why, if anything was due me at all, it should be $5.00. Will you please explain to me why this amount is all that is due me and why I am not entitled to a pension on account of my husband's death?[62]

In response to Alice's letter of October 8, 1924, she was informed of the reason for the five dollars she received:

I have to advise you that the check for $5.00 sent to you was in payment of the pension which accrued between January 4, 1923, the date of last payment to the soldier, and January 6, 1923, inclusive, the date of his death, or three days' pension at the rate of $50.00 per month....This was all the pension due and unpaid in the soldier's case at the time of his death, and as you were not married to him prior to June 27, 1905, and as his death was plainly not due to any disability incurred in his military *service, you are not entitled to a widow's pension under any existing law. This claim for pension filed by you on January 2, 1924, was not a claim for widow's pension, but was a claim for accrued pension; and it would be entirely useless for you to file a widow's claim.*[63]

It included two handwritten letters and letters sent by Senator Lewis B. Schwellenbach and Representative John M. Coffee, both of Washington State, to the Veterans Administration's chief of claims. A letter from the Dependents Claim Service apprised the Congressman of the Act of 1920:

Inasmuch as Mrs. Scott did not marry the veteran until June 26, 1911, she could have no title to pension as his widow under the Action of May 1, 1920, for the reason that marriage prior to June 27, 1905, is a condition to title to pension based on the veteran's service under any existing law unless she could furnish evidence to show that his death was the result of his military service in line of duty.[64]

Her application was rejected. She lived to March 1944 in Tacoma, Washington.

Walter's descendants, two great-grandchildren, are living in Washington.

WALLA WALLA COUNTY

JAMES CARL ABELL

October 1817–April 14, 1888
Lebanon, Marion County, Kentucky—Walla Walla City, Washington
McCool Catholic Church Cemetery (Defunct)
Walla Walla, Walla Walla County, Washington
Private, Company C, 125th Regiment, United States Colored Infantry
March 26, 1865–December 20, 1866
Louisville, Kentucky—Louisville, Kentucky

James C. Abell[65] was born in October 1817 in Marion County, Kentucky, into the ownership of William Madison Abell.[66]

Catholic priest Father James Quinn of Louisville, Kentucky, performed the marriage ceremony between James Abell and Rebecca Smith on July 26, 1846. They were the parents of Joseph, Lloyd, James, Anna and Laura.

He joined Company C of the 125th and was called to duty at Johnson's Island, Ohio; Cairo, Illinois; and lastly Leavenworth, Kansas, before assignment at Fort Union, New Mexico. The 125th U.S. Colored Infantry marched overland from Kansas to Santa Fe and scattered its companies among the forts of New Mexico.[67]

Besides Texans, residents of New Mexico were the only westerners who had seen garrisons of Black soldiers before the regulars arrived. The 125th U.S. Colored Infantry, the last volunteer regiment to muster out, had marched there from Fort Leavenworth, Kansas, in the spring of 1866. Although the press in New Mexico was not as uniformly hostile as the Texas press, one army officer found residents of the territory "musch [*sic*] disgusted at the idea of Negro troops being sent down there," fearing that they would not afford "any protection from the Indians."[68]

They stayed at Fort Union until July 1866 before moving to Fort McRea, New Mexico, for nine months of garrison duty. Living conditions at the fort were somewhat comfortable. The barracks that held one company measured 120 by 127 feet, with several windows on two sides of the building, and heating from the cold was provided by one stove. Single beds were made of iron.[69] The soldiers were responsible for keeping travelers safe along the Jornada del Muerto (Journey of the Dead) from marauding Indians. In September, a report by the commanding officer told of four soldiers herding stock attacked by treaty Indians; one soldier, Charles Quinn, was killed.

Company C, on May 17, 1867, moved to Fort Craig to perform escort and garrison duty. This lasted until October, when the company moved to Albuquerque, New Mexico, before heading to Fort Leavenworth, Kansas, for mustering out in December and returning to Louisville, Kentucky.

After a few years in Kentucky, the Abell family moved to Shawnee County, Kansas, to work the land—Rebecca was a weaver by profession. By late 1887, James, Rebecca and two of their grandchildren were living in Walla Walla, Washington. It was in Walla Walla that James lost his life on January 9, 1888, to pneumonia and the aftereffects of the Civil War, which plagued him for many years. He suffered from exposure from bad weather, inedible food and harsh living conditions, causing him to report to the government doctors a case of rheumatism.[70]

When James applied for his pension, he needed individuals to confirm his health prior to deterioration. In the report, the examiner gives his decision for using the slave owner's family description:

> [Albert J. Abell] *testifies* [he] *knew the claimant from childhood, he was formerly a slave and belonged to respondent's father, that for the five years previous to and at time of his enlistment Mar. 1865 he was a stout, healthy man and free from rheumatism or any other sickness, saw claimant about six months after he was discharged, about Christmas 1866 and he then apparently was well and healthy, but he broke fast after he got home, and he heard of his being there in bed with rheumatism, saw him in fall of 1870 and he was then suffering with rheumatism in*

his arms, wrist and legs and they were much swollen at this time and says he was about one-quarter disabled for manual labor from 1866 to 1861 by reason of rheumatism.

[Mary Abell] *testifies, claimant was formerly a slave and belonged to her husband, that previous to his enlistment he was perfectly sound and had been since his boyhood, knows nothing about his having the rheumatism on his return from the army, did not see claimant more than once in two months after his return, and as he was not much of a hand to complain of trouble, he did not have had rheumatism and she not know it.*

From the evidence before me [examiner Haswell] *I am of the opinion that this claim is meritous and that prior soundness is fully established, and I recommend its admission further examination being unnecessary.*[71]

James was approved for six dollars on March 10, 1886. After his death, Rebecca applied for the widow's pension while living in Washington State. She was approved and received twelve dollars per month until her death, on November 26, 1909.[72]

Rebecca stayed in Walla Walla for the next few years prior to moving to Denver, Colorado. Since their mother's death, James William and Anna

Seattle animal pounder. *Courtesy of Museum of History and Industry (MOHAI).*

had been their grandmother Rebecca's constant traveling companions. Rebecca spent several years living near her son Joseph, helping him during his illnesses.

By 1902, the family were once again in the state of Washington, residing in the city of Seattle but leaving their son Joseph in Denver. He died in 1904 and left no descendants.

The 1903 Seattle City Directory showed their residence at 820 21st Avenue South. The household included grandson James William, his wife and their two children; granddaughter Anna; and James C. Abell's, widow, Rebecca. The address changed to 822 21st Avenue South.[73] During his early years in Seattle, grandson James William Abell started work at the Seattle Police Department as an assistant pound master in 1908 and remained there until his retirement in 1928.[74] Photographers Webster and Stevens on September 14, 1921, took a picture of James when the newspaper reported he captured a stray coyote atop a Westlake Avenue building in Seattle.[75]

James W. remained in Seattle until his death on March 3, 1961. He survived his wife, Bertha Pearson Abell (died in 1931), his only son, James W.C. (died in 1922) and his sister Anna (died in 1909). He was buried at Holyrood Cemetery in Shoreline, Washington (just north of Seattle), while his grandmother Rebecca Abell and his sister Anna are buried at Calvary Cemetery in Seattle's University of Washington District.

There are no remaining direct descendants of James C. Abell. He has an unmarked grave in a defunct Catholic cemetery in Walla Walla, Washington.

YAKIMA COUNTY

JASPER P. (JONES) EVANS

March 8, 1846–December 9, 1927
Fredericktown, Mississippi—Yakima, Yakima County, Washington
Tahoma Cemetery
Yakima, Yakima County, Washington
Private, Company K, 18ᵗʰ Regiment, United States Colored Infantry
September 26, 1864–February 21, 1866
St. Louis, Missouri—Huntsville, Alabama

In a handwritten document dated December 27, 1901, Jasper explained his usage of two names when signing documents:

> *I inlisted under the name of Jasper E. Jones as my Boss was named Jones and my father was named Alford Evans. So since the war I have droped the old masters name and youse my father name Evans. I have not changed my name. The E. was put in my name insted of Evans or for Evans and as I inlisted with the old masters name attached to my name I could not send to the government and leave the Jones out in regard to my taxes. I have the old master name out as I no more a Slave befor the war. A collord man could not go in his father name he had to go in his Boss or master name unless they both belong to the same man.*[76]

Health concerns started in the fall of 1864, when he noticed bleeding from the rectum. The camp's doctor treated him for piles. Jasper said, "[C]ontracted of Piles. I bleed in Nashville and I Bleed in Chattenoga tn booth and I did not know that it was piles, I just thought that it was flux. So I yoused saave and it got better for a while and when on hoods rade [December 17–28]."[77]

It was during this conflict in January 1865 that Jasper was shot in the leg. An examining physician noted this when he applied for his pension.

After the war, Jasper moved to St. Louis, Missouri, and married Nancy Jane Hunter on November 25, 1869. The couple had one child, Alfred Evans. The marriage was short-lived. He applied for a divorce from Nancy on March 7, 1884. In the dissolution of Jasper's marriage, the defendant's failure to appear in court resulted in a decision by the court to grant Jasper's petition, and all court costs fell to Nancy.[78] The next month, Jasper married nineteen-year-old Belle C. Ballard of St. Charles County, Missouri, in the city of Alton in Madison County, Illinois, on April 9, 1884. Edward Noonan, justice of the peace, performed the ceremony. The family spent the next nine years in St. Louis, Missouri, before moving to Bucoda, Thurston County, Washington. They spent five years in the city of Centralia, Lewis County, Washington, arriving there in about 1898. While still living in Bucoda, Jasper applied for his pension using the service-connected health issue of piles. Three physicians examined Jasper and found that he had just seven decayed teeth left, suffered from swollen tonsils and had external bleeding piles. He was granted his pension.

In a statement from Henry Williams dated June 23, 1899, he confirmed that Jasper and his family left for Winlock, Washington, in 1893. He had known Jasper when they first met at Spanish Lake in Missouri in 1869.

In 1903, Belle had taken in William C. Phillips as a lodger to supplement the family's income. She became his caregiver until his death in 1906.

Taking advantage of the 1862 Homestead Act, Jasper was granted 160 acres in the Yakima Valley.[79] He also purchased his home at 803 North 2nd Street. They raised their family of eight children on that farm. Taking care of his family and running a farm became harder as the years progressed. By 1922, he had become incapacitated and applied for admission to the State Soldiers Home in Orting, Washington. The doctors determined that he would be bound to his bed.[80] His application was approved on January 8, 1923. He wanted Belle to move in with him, but the only beds available were in the ward. He also applied for admission to the hospital at Retsil Veterans Home in Port Orchard, Washington; admission was granted, but

Jasper Evans and family.
Courtesy of Yakima Valley Museum.

he did not move because the only beds available for him and his wife were in the hospital wards. He stayed at the hospital at Orting. While there, Jasper was examined two times within three months, once by his own personal physician, Dr. Edna Dale, and the second examination by the physician of the State Home Hospital. Both confirmed Jasper's medical condition. Dr. Edna Dale determined on September 21, 1926:

> *That JASPER E. EVANS has been paralyze since July 6, 1923 and has been totally helpless ever since that day; that he has no use at all of one side of his body, hence is totally helpless now will continue to be so.*[81]

A note in a medical examination by Dr. F.N. Bush dated December 16, 1926, confirmed his total incapacitation.

Jasper stayed an inmate of the state hospital until, for some unknown reason, he discharged himself on March 11, 1927. He died on December 9, 1928, at home. A will left by Jasper Evans gave his wife, Belle, his entire estate consisting of 160 acres of land and two lots in the city of North Yakima. He left nothing to his children.

It was now Belle's turn to maneuver the ins and outs of the Veterans Department. She applied for widow's pension on January 24, 1928, with the condition that she supply the following documents to the department: a verified copy of marriage certificate (a copy is unsatisfactory as evidence) and a verified copy of death certificate of Jasper's first wife, Jennie, or affidavit from her son, Alfred. Her certificate was approved on November 17, 1928, and her pension was set at a rate of thirty dollars per month. She solicited the help of the American Red Cross to get an increase in her widow's pension. She lived to 1955.

Jasper and Belle left many descendants in Washington.

ALLIN ALFRED HAWKINS

February 4, 1845–September 25, 1913
Huntington, Carroll County, Tennessee—Yakima, Yakima County, Washington
Tahoma National Cemetery
Yakima, Yakima County, Washington
Private, Company B, 13th Regiment, United States Colored Infantry
September 1, 1864–January 10, 1866
Jacksonville, Tennessee—Nashville, Tennessee

Born under the ownership of Isaac R. Hawkins, Allin Alfred lived with his master until his departure to enter the Union army, while his owner also decided that his duty was to join the same army.

After discharge from the service, Allen moved around for a few years. He stayed in Murray, Kentucky, for six years working as a tobacco picker; moved on to Illinois to work in the coal mines; farmed in Iowa; went back to Illinois to work the coal mines again; arrived in Kittitas County around 1889 and worked as a miner; and, finally, moved to Yakima, Washington, to farm. In between his travels, he stopped in Missouri and married Annie Harris. They had three children; two lived to adulthood.

In 1892, he applied for his Civil War pension, and it was granted. He explained the reasons for his disability:

> *That some time during the years 1881 or 1882 while working in a coal mine at Rapid City Illinois I was hurt in the back by lifting and since that I have*

50

suffered from a weak back and have been unable to do more than two kinds of a mans work. I further declare that on the fifth day of July 1894 I was accidentally shot in the left breast by a bullet from a 22 calibre rifle, the bullet striking near the collar bone and following the breast bone until it struck the left shoulder that since that time my left arm has been useless and that I believe the injury to be permanent and that I am disabled to such an extent by reason of said gunshot wound that I cannot perform more than one third of a mans work. I further declare that said disabilities are not due to vicious heabet.[82]

Hawkins became one of the wealthiest African Americans in the Yakima Valley. He obtained his wealth through hard work and farming of his land. The major crop grown by Hawkins was hops. He purchased a home and the Day Hops Ranch. The *Seattle Republican* newspaper dated October 19, 1906, reported that "the Sunnyside farmer, raised twenty five tons from eighteen acres, six acres of which was first year. His crop estimated to be worth $25,000."

Hawkins obtained his land through the Homestead Act of 1862, which granted 160 acres to a single man and 320 acres to a married couple. In his case, he only received 160 acres. In addition to the land, he obtained water rights to the property for $1,550 from Washington Irrigation Company on November 10, 1904.

By January 27, 1905, Hawkins and his wife had built a new home in the Yakima Valley. The *Seattle Republican* reported that "his new home…is one of the best advertisements the Sunnyside country ever had to tell what a poor man can do if he has the push." He and his wife had purchased a piano for the new home. Unfortunately, when moving the piano, it fell from a wagon and was broken into many pieces.

Allin Alfred and Anna Hawkins, from the *Seattle Republican. Courtesy of Library of Congress.*

New home of Allin and Anna Hawkins, from the *Seattle Republican. Courtesy of Library of Congress.*

Months later, the *Republican* authored an extensive article about Hawkins:

> [I]*t would do them good to visit the hop ranch of A.A. Hawkins, a stalwart "black" man, who was born a slave, and note the prosperous air that prevails thereon. First of all he has just about completed a ten room dwelling house for himself of the latest modern type, which is lighted from garret to cellar with acetylene gas, piped for a hot water plant, baths and toilets. It already has a telephone, thus giving him speaking communication with the outside world—in short, the home is the equal in every particular of the $3,000 city house. Mr. Hawkins has horses, cattle, sheep, swine and poultry galore and…great ricks of hay, field of potatoes and best of all his entire this year's hop.*[83]

The Hawkinses were known to entertain in the new home. The *Republican* noted that "a lavish engagement party [was] given for their son and Miss Bedell."

His prosperity would not last long. The failure of the hops market and falling victim to a swindle by Charles M. Scott slowly ate away at his fortune. Hawkins, to prevent complete loss of his fortune, had enlisted the aid of

Scott, cashier at the First National Bank of Sunnyside and president of Western Real Estate and Investments Company, to help him quit-claim forty acres to his son Luther Hawkins. Scott took advantage of the situation to misrepresent the documents that both Hawkins and Luther signed. At the conclusion of the transaction, Scott reassigned ownership of the land, sold the land to four individuals and mortgaged the land for $1,200 payable by Hawkins's son.

The Washington State Superior Court for the county of Yakima heard a case involving the same forty acres plus ninety additional acres. On February 15, 1907, J.B. George sued Hawkins and his wife, Anna, for $830.90 and won. To pay the sum, his acreage was auctioned off on the steps of the county courthouse on November 2, 1907. In the end, the land was now in the hands of another, and the Hawkins family were denied the return of that land.

Hawkins solicited lawyer John H. Lynch to sue Scott for the return of his land. The decision on September 24, 1913, by Judge Thomas Grady returned the land to Hawkins. The newspaper headlines for that day reported, "Land Restored to Aged Negro." The next day, Hawkins was dead. The *Yakima Morning Herald* reported on September 26, 1913, "Aged Negro Drops Dead—A.A. Hawkins, Civil War Veteran Overexerts Himself in His Pleasure at Recovery of Property."

Scott disappeared, and the local police had no idea where he had gone. It should be noted that Scott found his way to the city of Floras in Curry County, Oregon, according to the 1920 federal census, and was employed as a miner. He listed himself as "widowed."

After the death of her husband, Annie Hawkins and son Luther moved to Seattle temporarily until her eventual move to Ellensburg, Washington. As his wife, she received $11.73 on November 13, 1915—her accrued benefit of his final pension payment.

There are no living descendants of Allin Alfred Hawkins in Washington.

SPENCER T. JACKSON

August 12, 1844–November 19, 1916
Nickelsville, Fayette County, Kentucky—Seattle, King County, Washington
Lake View Cemetery
Seattle, King County, Washington

Private, Company A, 12th United States Colored Heavy Artillery
July 15, 1865–April 24, 1866
Nelson, Kentucky—Louisville, Kentucky

Spencer T. Jackson was born to John and Ellen Thurston Jackson of Kentucky. In his deposition of October 9, 1885, he explained his living conditions prior to joining the Union Army: "For five years before my enlistment I lived in Fayette Co. Ky 12 miles southeast of Lexington on Russel Pike. I was a slave and belonged to Daniel Bryant, was still lived on the old place in 1867." Daniel Bryant owned Spencer, his mother and one brother. In Bryant's affidavit dated June 1888, he confirmed his ownership of Jackson and his family:

> *I was a resident of Fayette County, Ky all my life up to 1865. I know the claimant, Spencer Jackson. I bought him when he was a baby, along with his mother, and I owned him until about the conclusion of the war, when he run away. His mother and family went before he did. No other member of our family owned a colored man by the name of Spencer Jackson. He was about 16 years of age when he left me and I think this was in 1864....I owned Reuben, but his other brother was owned about 5 miles from me.*[84]

Spencer's service in the Civil War was uneventful. The regiment never took part in any battles against the Confederates. The men spent their time at Camp Nelson and Bowling Green practicing for war. Their practiced skirmishes were held often. It was at one of these skirmishes that, Spencer recalled, he suffered his eventual blindness:

> *At Fort Sand Ky in May 1865, we were on a skirmish drill, shamming with blank cartridges. The officers had us divided in squads and we were placed in the bushes and briare and ordered to charge up to each other "firing at will," and as it was so smokey and the undergrowth was so thick we could not see each other so readily. And the man who was afronting me fired when we were in contact with each other and the discharge of his gun burnt my face and eyes. The boys said it was Barney Stewards gun that burnt me, for I did not see any afterwards.*[85]

He used this disabling injury to obtain his pension from the pension bureau. He originally received six dollars in pension payments. Up until a few days before his death, payment was twenty-five dollars per month. His road to his pension had its ups and downs. Every year he applied for increase in his pension because of his disability of his eyes and rheumatism, but to his dismay, he was often rejected for the simple reason that he had not obtained the age associated with pension laws. He also complained that he contracted rheumatism and got a hernia: "[A]nd is also suffering from Rheumatism which was brought on by exposure by sleeping in swamps at same place in 1865 and is also suffering from hernia in right groin which was incurred while lifting a field piece or old cannon, and while engaged in removing rubbage was caught under the old cannon which caused hernia in right groin. This occurred at Columbia, Kentucky in the latter part of the year 1865."[86]

After the war, Spencer returned to Kentucky and worked a few months for his former slave owner in Bourbon County, Kentucky. The southern summer heat and sunshine exacerbated the injury to his eyes. According to a statement given by his brother, John, on December 10, 1892, "He lived with me and remained there until 1868 (two years) and during that time he was suffering with Rheumatism and weak eyes, and in the spring of 1867, he was very bad and was compelled to take to his bed."[87]

Other siblings were solicited by Spencer to defend his martial status and his health issues. His brother, John, provided additional information:

> *John S. Jackson (brother)*
> …[W]*hen the claimant (my brother) came home from his discharge from the Army in the Spring of 1866, one year after the close of the War. He was very Lame and complained of great pain in his Hips, Back and Shoulder, his eyes were weak inflamed and blood shot, he lived with me for about one and one half years and during that he was compelled to employ a physician Dr. Jasper who treated him more than once.*[88]

Spencer moved to Belpre, Ohio, in 1869 and remained there for the next twenty-four years. During that time, he married Marie Jane Peyton on July 3, 1869. They had nine children. Even though he was in a different climate, he suffered with health issues he attributed to the war.

Sisters Sarah (Jackson) Thomas and Viva (Jackson) Turner were

> *familiar with his life and know that the said Spencer Jackson was married twice only. He was married the first time to Maria Allen, and she died in January 1902 in Portland Oregon. After the death of his first wife Spencer*

Jackson was not again married until he was married to Leatha L. Rice, the
present widow and claimant.[89]

In about 1892, he and his wife and four of his children moved to Calcasieu Parish, Louisiana.[90] They stayed in Louisiana until about 1900 before moving to Portland, Oregon. In Oregon, his wife, Maria, passed away on January 21, 1902. Three years later, Spencer married Leathe Logan Rice (former wife of Barney Rice) on June 24, 1905, and lived at 573½ Raleigh Street.

Spencer and Leathe moved to North Yakima, Washington, in November 1906. They spent a few years in Yakima County, where he obtained 160 acres of farmland through the Homestead Act of 1862 on August 28, 1911.[91] The *Yakima Herald* dated February 16, 1910, interviewed Spencer about drilling outfits above Selah Gap:

> *S. T. Spencer, who is a homesteader in township 13, but who to get in from*
> *his homestead has to traverse a large portion of township 14, came to North*
> *Yakima last evening. He had driven 20 miles and say in that time he saw*
> *at least six drilling outfits at work. There is great interest, he says, among*
> *all the people out in the sagebrush.*[92]

After the death of Spencer, Leathe married a Mr. Coleman of Yakima; this was her third marriage. They moved back to Yakima from Seattle. When Leathe was informed of the death of Spencer, she petitioned the court to manage his estate, as he died intestate. The probate records for Spencer were found in the state archives for Yakima County, Washington. Leathe Coleman was assigned as executrix of his estate by court order. Each of his surviving children inherited $18.02. Leathe sold the land for $800 to Howard T. Nye; the land was described as "unworked farmland." She paid the expenses of the estate, and the balance of $584 was given as her share of the estate.

Spencer left many descendants in Seattle.

WILLIAM CALVIN PHILLIPS

February 10, 1833 November 14, 1906
Carmichaels, Greene County, Pennsylvania—Yakima, Yakima County, Washington
Tahoma National Cemetery
Yakima, Yakima County, Washington

Company E, 60th United States Colored Infantry,
(formerly 1st Iowa Colored Volunteers)
First Sergeant, Company E, 60th Regiment, United States Colored Infantry
August 21, 1863–October 15, 1865
Keokuk, Iowa—Duvalls Bluff, Arkansas

This soldier was found while reviewing the pension record for Augustus M. Dixon. Within Dixon's pension file were two depositions that mentioned William Calvin Phillips: a deposition from Belle Evans, wife of Jasper Evans, and a deposition from Phillips himself:

> *During the first six months of 1864, the unit performed garrison duty, scouted the nearby countryside and Mississippi islands, and performed fatigue duty plus unloading supply ships, driving teams, and building fortifications. On January 29, for example, Iowa Companies A thru D remained in camp while Company E was protecting government wood choppers on Island No. 55 and Company F (along with the St. Louis companies G through K) relieved a white Missouri regiment at garrison duty, engaged in artillery drill, and built and repaired batteries and rifle pits.*[93]

The 60th U.S. Colored Infantry performed one last task before dispersing back into civilian life. On October 31, 1865, the men held a "Convention of Colored Iowa Soldiers" at Davenport's Camp McClellan to add their collective voice to the movement for suffrage reform. Their "address to the people of Iowa" asserted that "he who is worthy to be trusted with the musket can and ought to be trusted with the ballot."[94]

William did a lot of traveling after his army service. For the next twenty-one years, he traveled through six states: Illinois, Nebraska, Colorado, Kansas, New Mexico and Arizona. William's first marriage occurred while he was traveling through Illinois. On August 14, 1959, he married Miss Juliana McGill. She passed away five years later in February 1864 in Iowa. His second marriage, in 1878, was to Mary Smith Meaddows while in Ashland, Nebraska. They had two children: a daughter, Edith, born in Nebraska and a son, Fernando Scott Phillips, born in 1880 in Topeka, Kansas. By 1886, his wife, Mary, had applied for divorce while they were living in New Mexico, and it was granted.

Phillips moved from Colorado to Washington and back to Iowa. In Iowa on June 27, 1894, he made his initial application for his Civil War pension. He claimed total disability due to rheumatism and disease of the heart.

While he waited to hear about his application, he became ill and was admitted to the Colorado Soldiers and Sailors Home in Monte Vista. The local physician, Dr. W.A. Packard, treated him for chronic bronchitis and rheumatism. He also noted that "by reason of the disabilities as named, he is three fourths disabled in the performance of manual labor." His records from the home stated that he discharged himself on July 22, 1898, and moved to Durango.[95]

On February 10, 1901, he was admitted to the Washington State Soldiers Home at Orting for a rapidly deteriorating health problem. Examination by the home's physician found myriad health issues: swollen joints, a thick coating on his tongue, disease of the eyes due to cataracts, chronic diarrhea, catarrh of the throat and tonsils, a cut on his ankle and bronchitis. He explained the cut on the foot he sustained while cutting wood with an axe during his time in the army. He did not stay long at the home; he discharged himself on November 15, 1898, and moved to North Yakima, Washington.

In many of his physical examinations, he complained that his case of rheumatism and contracting typhoid fever was a result of spending time in damp conditions during the war. Margaret E. Breckinridge, a nurse during the war who worked at a hospital in Helena, Arkansas, described the situation in that city:

> *You never saw so wretched a place as Helena; low damp, and enveloped in a continual fog, the rain poured down the whole time we were there, and the camps stretching for miles up and down the river looked like the constant and abiding dwelling-place of fever and ague, and it is without doubt a most sickly post, and why it is held still though known and proved to be a most unhealthy place, nobody seems able or willing to tell.*[96]

In Yakima, he purchased some land and probably did some farming but soon decided that he could not work to sustain the farm. He stayed at Belle Evans's home, known to be a good place to board, while he slowly deteriorated from his health issues. He lived with the Evans family until his death on November 14, 1906. Other former Civil War soldiers soon found themselves meeting at the Evans home. Alfred Hawkins, Jasper Evans, Augustus Dixon and William Phillips all lived in the same North Yakima community.

Phillips was granted his pension in 1906 for just a few months.

At the time of Phillips's death, he had no will. H.B. Doust petitioned the court to administer Phillips's estate. It consisted of nine-tenths of an acre of land with a small house and a one-fortieth share of Old Union Ditch Company with a total value of $1,400.00. The property was sold at an open auction on the courthouse stairs for $600, and the stock was sold for $875. Belle Evans, a creditor, was approved by the court and paid $90.

Meade Post 9 of the Grand Army of the Republic paid for the funeral services for Phillips and was reimbursed by his estate.

William C. Phillips left no living descendants in Washington or Kansas.

PART II

WESTERN WASHINGTON

KING COUNTY

GIDEON H. "STUMP" BAILEY

June 30, 1838–July 3, 1905
Dresden, Kent County, Ontario, Canada—Seattle, King County, Washington
Grand Army of the Republic (GAR) Cemetery
Seattle, King County, Washington
Corporal, Company C, 6th Regiment, United States Colored Infantry
September 15, 1865–September 20, 1866
Elmira, New York—Wilmington, North Carolina

Gideon H. "Stump" Bailey was born in 1838 to James and Margaret Stump in Kent County in the Province of Ontario, Canada. His parents were born in Tennessee and Haiti, respectively, and as far as it can be determined, this family fled to Canada from Tennessee just shortly after the birth of his sister Maria in 1830. Also born to this family was Enoch Stump in 1837 in Canada. Both Gideon and Enoch married in 1861—Gideon to Charlotte and Enoch to Sarah J.

After Gideon joined Company C of the 6th Regiment, he became very ill with a severe cold that the doctors later diagnosed as pneumonia. From September 20 to September 25, 1865, the doctors confined him to the field hospital in Elmira, New York. Fort Harrison was his new duty station on October 6 along with four hundred other new recruits—they had just missed a very bloody battle at New Market Heights, Virginia. He was promoted to corporal on January 31, 1865.

Soldier's military pension card. *Courtesy of Ancestry.com.*

After mustering out of the service, Gideon moved to Detroit, Michigan, and married Henrietta Childs on December 8, 1868.[97] In Detroit, he worked as a porter for twenty-five dollars per month. This job was short-lived because it required going up and down stairs; shortness of breath caused by the war hampered his ability to do his job adequately.

In a medical examination, a pension doctor described the physical features of this former Canadian sailor, noting that he had an anchor and a cutlass tattoo on his right forearm and an anchor on his left forearm. They found no defects attributed to the war.

In June 1876, Gideon married for a third time in Illinois to the former Mary Elizabeth Kendricks Cook. She brought into the marriage four children by a slave relationship and two from a previous marriage.

Bailey came to Franklin, Washington, from Braidwood, Illinois, in about 1889 to work in the coal mines as a strikebreaker and as a "mine carpenter." The armed convoy of strikebreakers and guards arrived in Roslyn on August 21, 1888. Initially, they made camp at a mine just outside Roslyn, near the present-day town of Ronald. Their families would later join the Black miners, thus completing what was up to that time the largest increase in Washington Territory's African American population. They immediately constructed a barricade of logs and barbed wire around their encampment to deter attacks by the striking miners.[98]

An Indianapolis newspaper, the *Freeman*, dated August 15, 1891, reported more information on the strike in Franklin:

> *The white strikers whose places were filled by colored miners at Franklin, Wash., have by a system of bulldozing and intimidation harassed and annoyed the boys considerably; not being satisfied with this, they secretly planned to assassinate them. Fortunately, their intentions were suspected and*

Lime Kiln Club, Black Miners Association, circa 1890–1910. *Courtesy of Renton Historical Museum.*

> *their coming awaited; they came. Results: three killed and many dangerously wounded; the Afro-Americans escaped totally uninjured and unscratched.*

During the five or six years he lived and worked in Franklin, he helped organize the Republican Club and became an early backer of the *Seattle Standard* newspaper. By 1891, Gideon had become the first president of the Washington State Afro-American League and in 1894 became the first African American appointed justice of the peace of Franklin by the county commissioners.

Gideon Bailey's judicial activities included the following, as reported in the May 2, 1894 *Seattle Post-Intelligencer*:

> *Williams and "Ginger" escaped from the guardhouse, but the former was recaptured. Both were brought before Justice of Peace Gideon Bailey, who sent Dawsey to jail for ninety days and fined Williams $50 and costs. Charles Williams, colored, was returned at the county jail yesterday from Franklin to serve out fifty days imposed by the Justice of Peace Bailey for resisting an officer.*[99]

Also, during his time in Franklin, he witnessed many mine disasters that occurred. In one such disaster on October 17, 1895, he was called on to join a coroner's jury to determine the reason for the death of four miners:

The accident was caused by August Johnson, who dropped his lamp, setting fire to the feeder of gas. Instead of throwing a shovelful of dirt on it to put it out, he ran down the slope to get the pit foreman. While he was bringing the help the timbers caught fire and five lengths of brattice work were ablaze and the smoke became so intense as to prevent getting at it. Finding that the fire could not be extinguished the four men named volunteered to go down and close a door between the main and auxiliary slope....Johnson states that he tried to fight the fire with his coat.[100]

The coroner's jury of six men determined:

That the deceased, George W. Smalley, age 32 years; John H. Glover, age 26 years; John Adams, aged 28 years, and James Stafford, aged 39 years, were natives of America, and that the above parties and each of them came to their death by suffocation in the Franklin mine on the 17th of October, 1895, about the hour of 12 o'clock a.m. of said day, in said county of King, state of Washington, and that they voluntarily went into said mine and without any orders from the Oregon Improvement Company, or any of its agents, servants or employees.[101]

What was left of those men was recovered on December 12, 1895. The news reported, "Nothing was found but blackened bones and the remains were identified by articles known to be on the bodies of such as a watch, two keys and a ruler."[102]

In the year 1897, Bailey and Con A. Rideout, Prince Hall Masons, contacted the Grand Lodge of Washington about allowing Bailey's group and the Grand Lodge a way of communicating with each other. After making a thorough study of the subject, the committee decided unequivocally that "Prince Hall Freemasonry was therefore a legitimate order."[103] Washington Lodge 49, created in Franklin, Washington, later moved to Seattle, Washington.

After living in Franklin, Washington, for many years, Gideon and his wife, Mary, moved to Beacon Hill in Seattle. Here, he continued his active involvement with the Republican Club, the Masons, the Phylaxis Society and the John Miller Post of the Grand Army of the Republic. He also became a much-requested lecturer.[104]

Shortly after Gideon's death, his wife applied for his Civil War pension on July 25, 1905. She encountered some of the same difficulties that most African American former Civil War soldiers' wives encountered: lack of birth, death and marriage certificates. In Mary's case, she needed to produce

Gideon's previous wife Henrietta's date of death.[105] With Mary's lack of reading and writing skills, as stated in her deposition, "she always depended on her husband to do all the writing and correspondence because she can't read and write herself."[106]

She even had to produce proof of her divorce from her first husband, Norbin Cook. The Court of Illinois produced the divorce decree. In the document, her divorce was granted on the grounds of her husband's "habitual drunkenness two years prior to filing…extreme and repeated cruelty and wholly unfit to have the care, custody and control or education of children."[107] The divorce was granted on May 8, 1876. She and Gideon married in June of the same year.

Even though she inherited the home and some personal property, she testified before the pension examiner that "she has no income nor means of support…her husband left no life insurance and no money, and she is too old and feeble to work and has to depend upon the charity of her friends and kindly disposed people to provide her food and clothing."[108]

For some years after Gideon's death, Mary's granddaughter Lillian Murdock and family lived with Mary. It was during this time that Mary's health took a turn for the worse. Lillian had a difficult time taking care of her grandmother, working a twelve-hour shift and taking care of her own family. Lillian and the John Miller Post Corps requested Mary's admission to the Washington Veterans Home in Retsil, Kitsap County, Washington; she was granted admission on June 7, 1920. Mary lived at Retsil until her death on September 19, 1922, and is buried at the home's cemetery.[109]

You can find Gideon's burial plot and unique headstone at the Grand Army of the Republic Cemetery on Capitol Hill in Seattle, Washington. Each April, the Phylaxis Society celebrates his life.

Gideon and Mary had no children of their own.

Joseph P. Bennett

August 25, 1842–July 10, 1935
St. Kitts, British West Indies—Seattle, King County, Washington
Cremated, Place of Interment Unknown
Private, Companies B & H, 56th Massachusetts Volunteer Regiment
December 29, 1863–July 29, 1865
Berkley, Massachusetts—Readville, Massachusetts

Joseph is the first of two African Americans within this group of men who was not a member of the U.S. Colored Troops. He was a cook for an all-white regiment for Companies B and G of the 56th Massachusetts.[110] The regiment had three African Americans named by researcher and author Jacqueline Moss.[111]

Joseph P. Bennett was born in St. Kitts, British West Indies, on August 26, 1842. He left the islands when he was fourteen years old.

The *Seattle Republican*'s "Northwest Negro Progress Number" special edition, dated 1909, reported a brief history of Bennett: "He left home [West Indies] on a French ship, was kidnapped from it and put in prison by the

Joseph Penny Bennett, from the *Seattle Republican. Courtesy of Library of Congress.*

Confederates at New Orleans; was released by the intervention of the British consul, and immediately enlisted in the Union Army."[112]

Eugene Berwanger's book *The British Foreign Service and the America Civil War* discusses a situation similar to if not the same as Bennett's: "In July 1861, three West Indian sailors were taken from a Union merchant ship by a confederate privateer and were brought to New Orleans and imprisoned." Berwanger goes on to say that "negotiations between Consuls Mure and later Coppell and the Louisiana authorities finally lead to the sailors' release in January 1862. New Orleans police put them on a small craft and sent them into the Gulf of Mexico, where they were picked up by a United States warship."[113]

Even though Bennett stated that he "immediately enlisted," his enlistment papers state otherwise. Bennett's pension record verified his enlistment date of December 29, 1863, at Berkley, Massachusetts, and he was discharged on July 29, 1865, at Readville, Massachusetts.

After his discharge from the service, Bennett returned to the Massachusetts area to work as a sailor. For many years, Bennett spent his time on the sea—not giving any details as to where he was between 1870 and 1880. A look through his pension record showed that Joseph stated he spent some time in San Francisco, where he married twice.

The 1870 census for Boston, Massachusetts, listed Joseph Bennett with seventy-eight other men who identified themselves as "sailors," and they seemed to be living in the same rooming house operated by Thomas Carty and his wife.[114]

In the 1871 San Francisco City Directory, he was listed as a seaman working for the Northern Pacific Transportation Company on the SS *Pacific Steamer*. According to the same city directories, Bennett was in Oakland from 1872 to 1876 and in San Francisco from 1877 to 1883; he then returned to Oakland from 1884 to 1889. He worked as a cook in private homes and several hotels. Working as a seaman seemed to be seasonal; the city directories for those cities listed his occupation as "cook." It can only be assumed that he was at sea during the years he was missing from the city directories. For a few months in 1880, he was incarcerated in the City and County Industrial School (Male Department) for "petty larceny."[115]

He married his first wife, Emma Chance Wilson, on November 27, 1880, in San Francisco; she died on November 25, 1883, in San Francisco and was buried there. This couple had no children. Joseph Bennett met his second wife, Anna Bell Fountain, and then married her on June 25, 1884, in San Francisco.

By 1889, Bennett and his wife had moved to Seattle, where he found a job as janitor for Theodore Haller at an office and residence building named for Theodore's brother, George Morris Haller. It was found on 2nd Avenue and Columbia Street in downtown Seattle.[116] Bennett was a faithful employee of Haller's for nineteen years. At one point, Bennett was injured in an elevator accident, and Haller took care of his medical needs.[117] It was here that Bennett befriended another Civil War soldier, Samuel Johnson.

These two men worked side by side at the Haller Building until Johnson's death in 1912. Because of their friendship, Bennett petitioned the court to be assigned as executor of Johnson's estate and for the arrangement of funeral rights.

Bennett, like others in this writing, was a member of the Free Masons. He was one of the first members the Prince Hall Lodge No. 2 in Seattle. The John A. Mulligan Lodge No. 1 petitioned for a new lodge and granted Alexander Hester, Joseph Bennett and others the new lodge. On May 19, 1892, C.A. Rideout, Right Worshipful Deputy and Grand Master, and other grand officers dedicated and installed officers that included Hester as Worshipful Master and Bennett as Senior Warden.[118] This lodge was affiliated with the Prince Hall Masons of Illinois, not Seattle.

Bennett applied for his Civil War pension in 1905 and was required to be examined by the usual three medical professionals. In his examination on November 1, 1905, he complained of a strain of his lower back caused by lifting heavy items during the war. The effects of the Civil War were quickly catching up with him. The back ailment would follow him throughout his lifetime. It was so bothersome that by 1918, he could not continue his job

Mount Baker Theater (formerly Good Luck Theater). *Courtesy of Puget Sound Archives, Bellevue, Washington.*

as a janitor at the Haller Building. He was approved in March 1907 for a rate of $12. From that date until 1935, over twenty-five years, his pension increased to $100 per month. At his death, his son, Joseph M., received $33 as part of the accrued rate.

On the evening of June 2, 1930, Joseph P. Bennett's wife, Anna, spent some time at the Mount Baker Movie House (originally named Good Luck Theater) located at 24th and South Jackson Streets, to watch the latest movie. The movie house was within walking distance of her home, but Anna never made it home that evening; by the time she reached the steps of Rainier School at 23rd and South King Street, she had suffered a heart attack, and she died on those steps at 11:00 p.m. She was just four blocks away from her home at 23rd and South Charles Street.[119] Anna was sixty-two years old.

Sometime after the death of his wife, Bennett's health so deteriorated that he had to move in with his son for twenty-four-hour care. Joseph M. cared for his father from June 2, 1930, to July 8, 1935. In a statement from Joseph M.:

> *Since the death of claimant's wife (affiant's mother), claimant has constantly required affiant's personal care and attendance, claimant is... unable to care for himself. That claimant is not bed fast, but is confined to his house, and has been confined to his house since June 2, 1930.*[120]

70

On July 8, 1935, Joseph was admitted to U.S. Marine Hospital. When examined by doctors, his condition at admission was described as follows: "Skin cold, condition very weak and unconscious." He occupied room 705 for the next three days, after which he died at 4:40 p.m. on July 10, 1935. A full examination of Joseph was conducted the evening of his admission. The doctors concluded:

> *For the past year & half, the patient has been becoming more & more helpless in taking care of himself. His mind has been declining steadily over the period....For the past 6 weeks the patient has answered question by grunts, has eaten only when fed & has had incontinence of feces and of urine. Since 7-5-35 patient has made no sound & has eaten nothing but simply lies in bed staring blankly.* [121]

According to his autopsy report on the same day, there was a tattoo of a ship on his left arm, which showed that he might have traveled around Cape Horn, the southernmost tip of Chile, South America. In addition, the doctor concluded that Joseph died of generalized arteriosclerosis, arteriosclerotic nephritis, chronic adherent pericarditis, terminal bronchipneumonia involving both lungs and marked emaciation probably due to malnutrition. [122]

Joseph and Anna had one child, Joseph Morris Bennett, who survived to 1941; he left no additional descendants. Joseph M. was a problem child. In a short article in the March 24, 1900 *Seattle Post-Intelligencer*, "Joe Bennett a Bad Boy," it noted:

> *Joseph M. Bennett, colored, a small boy was committed to the reform school yesterday afternoon by Judge Benson in the superior court. Joseph P. Bennett, father of the little fellow, said that his son was a bad boy generally and would not go to school. Joseph, he said, takes pleasure in staying out nights, in places where his parents cannot find him. He had just turned 13 the month before he was committed.*

Joseph Bennett was cremated; his cremains have not been found. His body was processed by Angelus Funeral Home. To date, those records have not been found since the closing of that business.

HENRY CARPER

June 1846–August 7, 1920
Sussex County, Virginia—Seattle, King County, Washington
Mount Pleasant Cemetery
Seattle, King County, Washington
Private, Company I, 27th United States Colored Infantry
July 11, 1864–September 21, 1865
Mansfield, Ohio—Southville, North Carolina

Henry Carper, an eighteen-year-old, gray-eyed, light brown–haired, mulatto-complexioned former slave, entered the Civil War via enlistment in Mansfield, Ohio, on July 11, 1864, as a substitute for George McCree. When he was transferred to his unit of regular infantry on July 28, 1864, Henry was given the role of pioneer.[123] He completed his service in Smithville, North Carolina, on September 21, 1865. Carper experienced war two days after being assigned to the 27th Regiment. The men of the regiment spent the early hours watching the Battle of the Crater:

> *What ensued on July 30, 1864, at the Battle of the Crater was one of the most mismanaged tragedies of the war. The assault waves that did go in, leaderless and without orders, sought safety in the massive crater left by the explosion rather than pushing forward, thus giving Lee precious time to organize a defense and seal the breach. The brave men of the colored division watched with helpless rage and frustration as the chance to win… an overwhelming victory was tossed away.*[124]

The major battle for Henry Carper and his comrade Walter Scott[125] was the engagement at Fort Fisher.

> *The 27th U.S. Colored Troops participated in the mop-up operations against Fort Fisher on the night of January 15, 1865, and was involved in the initial surrender negotiations. At Fisher, the Ohio unit was one day shy of a year old, having been organized at Camp Delaware on January 16, 1864.…At Fisher, the 27th suffered a few casualties, including one killed and four wounded.*[126]

Henry, in a Seattle newspaper, recalled his time in the service:

> [He] *served in the Union army during the last years of the Civil War. He was in an Ohio regiment and tells a story of his early struggles. "When I mustered out, I didn't have a penny. I sold a pair of trousers for a dollar, spent 20 cents for something to eat and walked 300 miles to get a job. I worked in Knoxville, Tenn, and as fast as I got money, I put it into property and sold it when it rose in value."*[127]

After his discharge from service, he relocated to Knoxville, Tennessee, after traveling from Smithville, North Carolina. During his travels between 1865 and 1866, he met Lucy Jamison of Washington, D.C., a manumitted slave girl described in her manumission papers, dated April 16, 1862, as "age about 15 years, about four feet nine or ten inches tall, a mulatto, no particular marks remembered."[128] Henry and Lucy married on October 11, 1866, in the city of Fincastle in Botetourt County, Virginia. Two children quickly entered the family: Jennie in 1867 and Robert in 1868. Carper was a very industrious individual and established himself as a proprietor of a local saloon, Carper Saloon, along with his half-brother, Thomas Prince, as a barkeep. By 1880, Henry was living with his two children, Jennie and Robert; his mother, Rebecca Prince; and his stepfather Wilson Prince, but without Lucy.

It's estimated that Lucy left home between 1870 and 1880 and not of her own free will. According to a deposition taken from Lucy's aunt, Mary J. Smith, she overhead Henry telling Ella, his second wife:

> [Lucy] *was not satisfied with him and took up with another man.… [He] gave her a hundred dollars and put her on a train and sent her off to her people* [in Virginia]. *He also said he told her that he would take her back if she reformed…she never did…heard she married a preacher.*[129]

When Henry filed for a divorce, the local newspaper posted a notice that "Lucy Carper the defendant, is a non-resident of the State of Tennessee."[130] Lucy did not respond to the many notices posted in the local papers. The court granted the divorce in January 1886, thus making Henry a single man, and gave him custody of the two children. He wasted no time and purchased two train tickets and shipped his children to Ohio; Jennie went to school in Xenia and Robert to "Cincinnati, which will be his home in the future."[131] These children returned a few years later. Robert's return was noted in the local paper: "Robert Carper is in the city, returning from New Orleans instead of Cincinnati, as the Gazette said."[132]

Henry and Ella Carper
with grandson Robert.
*Photo in possession of
Douglas MacQuarrie.*

Lucy did go home to her family in Fincastle, Virginia. Lucy married Thomas Carrington in 1887 and Robert Gilliam in 1912. She died in 1917 of the grippe and was buried at Old City Cemetery in Lynchburg, Virginia.

Henry married Ella Virginia Richardson of Greenville, Tennessee, on April 1, 1886. The *Knoxville Journal* announced the return of the newlyweds from the wedding ceremony at the family home of Ella.

Acceptance by the colored community of Knoxville came quickly for this couple. Henry and Ella were invited to join many of the colored members of the community's special events of the city; there were parties at the homes of the elite they attended. A social committee enlisted Carper to help with preparations for a major event. Frederick Douglass, the great orator, was presenting "Self Made Men" at the Staub Theater, where a "greater portion of the auditorium will be reserved for the negroes."[133]

Even though Henry was well respected by the community, he was not without some humiliation from the misdeeds of his two sons, Robert and Harry. The local paper wrote of the troubled boys. Robert spent at least fifteen months in the penitentiary in Blount, Tennessee, for theft. Harry's addiction to drugs turned him into a skillful burglar.

Henry's intelligence helped him rise quickly through the ranks of hotel stewards to head waiter in the dining room of Hotel Hattie and later to the Imperial Hotel. When the Imperial Hotel needed renovation, the Black community purchased stock to renovate.[134]

Early on, Henry endeavored to establish himself as realtor. The purchase of 206 Main Street was the start of his rise in the community of Knoxville, Tennessee.

For nine months in 1903, Henry and Ella lived in Meadville, Pennsylvania. In the city directory entry for Henry and Ella, they were identified as "colored" and living at 285 North Street. This distinction is important, as sometime between his relocation from Pennsylvania to Seattle, they became "white." It may be that he took advantage of his light complexion and light eyes and hair, something he did not do in Knoxville. The census for 1880 reported that he was Black; the 1900 census reported that he was mulatto. The city directories in Knoxville either used small the letter "c" or an asterisk to denote the racial identity of certain citizens.

Like many old soldiers, he applied for his Civil War pension. This process was heavy with obstacles. Each man had to produce documents that former slaves did not have. If they were not able to produce those items, it was up to the old soldiers to obtain affidavits from individuals who corroborated their very existence: proof of births, marriages, divorces and deaths. If they could not produce those items, then individuals who knew them were deposed by the pension board examiners and their veracity rated. Then each man was examined by three government doctors to assess their health and their ability to do manual labor. Many of these soldiers complained of rheumatism from exposure to weather, loss of teeth from mushy gums (caused by scurvy), aftereffects of measles and partial blindness from blowback from gunpowder and flux, to name a few. Henry's maladies included "rheumatism and heart disease and corns on bottom of both feet impeding walking, weakness of back, disease of liver, stomach, bowels, rectum and piles, defective vision of both eyes."[135] He was awarded certificate no. 579802 on July 18, 1890, in Tennessee, thus allowing him to start receiving his pension of $35 starting in the third quarter of 1908. His pension progressively increased to $151.50 until the third quarter of 1920 and his death. His wife, Ella, received her widow's certificate on August 25, 1920, with a start date of the fourth quarter of 1921 and payment of $521.06, including a sum of money for a minor child, Charles. For the next nine months, Ella received $90 for herself and Charles. When Charles reached sixteen, the payment to Ella was reduced to $30 per month until her death in 1937.[136]

Once in Seattle, Henry used his knowledge of real estate to purchase his home at 155 Melrose Avenue North and their son Harry's home at 820 Ninth Street North. In Seattle, his transition to the white community came very easily. Henry retired in 1910 with lots of fanfare. The *Seattle Daily*

Times article "Henry Carper Gets His Share: Retires" described how he became successful:

> *The boys of the present day deserve a better chance to advance in the world than they are now getting. My belief is that when a man has got enough to live on comfortably, especially if he is getting along in years, he should step aside and let the boys have a chance....They deserve the same chance that their fathers had. The old men should retire if they can afford it.*[137]

He could afford his retirement and lived very comfortably. He owned a cottage on Melrose Avenue North and six other properties scattered around the Seattle area. Henry was "known among real estate men as one of the shrewdest and most successful investors in Seattle," despite the fact that "he came here from a small town in Pennsylvania with comparatively little money."[138]

It was not long before Henry's sons, Harry and Robert, were up to their usual antics. Harry's thefts were getting more brazen, and the size of the loot was getting larger. He even asked his wife, Maybelle, to join him. Harry was caught with the loot on two occasions, landing him in the Western State Reformatory in Monroe, Washington. For the first offence, he was sentenced on December 31, 1915, for burglary; his second offense was unlawful possession of narcotic drugs with intent to sell in 1924.[139] Harry was also incarcerated in Walla Walla Penitentiary of Washington State for a period of two years starting in 1924. His addiction to drugs eventually landed him in a hospital for the insane, where he died at age forty-eight.

Robert's encounters with the judicial system were frequent. During the years from 1883 to 1885, Robert was involved in many situations that included vagrancy, larceny and stealing expensive jewelry. Each illegal action resulted in incarceration in the workhouse or months in the county jails in Knoxville and Blountville, Tennessee. His father, Henry Carper, was present at Robert's trial for robbery in the Blountville court. Instead of bailing him out, Henry allowed the court to keep his son in jail.

Harry was given the name "master burglar" by the *Seattle Star* of October 8, 1919. It was so bad that his father wrote, on two occasions, about the dangers of addiction. In the October 14, 1919 edition of the *Seattle Daily Times* and *Seattle Post-Intelligencer*, Henry lamented:

> *I feel the public should know my son's training was all right; that his traits are not inherited; that, in a word, he was a Dr. Jekyll when he was without*

"dope," and a Hyde when using it....I reckon this might not be considered good taste by some for a father to describe his son as a thief and a liar; but I am doing it for the good of other parents. I have suffered and I don't want others to suffer from the same cause.[140]

The next day, the *Seattle Star* ran a story about Henry and the problems he had with Harry:

I am the father of Harry Carper, he said. My boy is a burglar. His mother is feeble and I am old. Today he faces a penitentiary sentence, despite the training of a good home. He stole to satisfy his awful craving for narcotics—he stole for drugs because he was a victim of the illusion that drugs were concealed everywhere.[141]

Henry can be described as a man of high standards and was a very moral man. He warned his neighbors of the bad acts of his son Harry and removed Robert from the household to prevent more illegal behavior. Even the removal of his first wife, Lucy, was a way of helping her to repent her errant behavior, with no success. His sons spent time incarcerated in local jails. Harry died in Western State Hospital in Steilacoom, Washington, an institution for the insane, and Robert was found guilty of murder and was removed to an institution for life in Ohio.

Henry joined the Stevens Post One of the Grand Army of the Republic (GAR). With pride he wore his membership lapel pin to their events. This organization for several Memorial Day events sent the "old Union soldiers," and later they added elderly Confederates soldiers, to the local schools to talk with the children about patriotism.[142]

Henry was well known for his philosophic opinion about the condition of his fellow colored men in Knoxville:

Now my brethren, there is reasons in all things, as in this. If you ever owed this debt—which at some time I can show you never have owed the Republican part, but to the Union army, full of good Democrats, and to yourselves, many of whom fought for their own freedom—I say if you ever did owe this debt solely to the Republican party, have we not about paid it? Now, let us look at it this way. A man who is not allowed to think as he pleases and to act upon his own convictions is the worst sort of a slave. He is such a slave as should not be found in the great land of "political and religious liberty, such as is claimed for the United States."[143]

When Henry Carper died, Ella explained in her deposition dated June 1, 1921, their arrangement regarding his/her estate:

[H]e made a will, but it was not placed on probate proceedings. He deeded his real estate to me before his death. I have his original will. We each made wills—one to the other—and held them and since his death, I have had the deeds he gave me recorded and destroyed those I made to him, that being in accordance with the arrangement and agreement between us.[144]

Henry Carper left several lines of descendants living in Washington, Michigan, Ohio, Tennessee and California with surnames of Carper, Prince, Hardin(en), Hargo, Alexander, Walker, Graham, Simpson, MacQuarrie and Carroll.

DAVID CLARK AND EDWARD CLARK

DAVID CLARK
July 12, 1838–October 20, 1921
Parkville, Clay County, Missouri—Seattle, King County, Washington
Lake View Cemetery
Seattle, King County, Washington

EDWARD CLARK
July 4, 1844–August 11, 1932
Parkville, Clay County, Missouri—Chicago, Cook County, Illinois
Grand Army of the Republic (GAR)
Seattle, King County, Washington
Private and Corporal, 1st Kansas Colored Volunteer Regiment,
Later Company F, 79th Regiment United States Colored Infantry
Topeka, Kansas—Fort Leavenworth, Kansas
August 16, 1862–November 3, 1865

Brothers David Clark and Edward Clark were slaves who ran away from their owners and joined the 1st Kansas Colored Volunteers, later known as the 79th U.S. Colored Infantry:

The men who filled up the companies of the First Kansas Colored Volunteers were largely recruited from among fugitive slaves out of Arkansas and Missouri. Some of them were fugitives in a technical sense only; their former owners complained bitterly, in some instances that Lane's marauders had stolen them out of hand, which was probably true.[145]

They fought in three major engagements: Island Mound, Honey Springs and Poison Springs. Their first battle and victory at Island Mound, Missouri, on October 29, 1862, proved that former slaves, now soldiers, could fight. The regiment sustained eight deaths and eleven wounded men. Losses to the enemy were fifteen to fifty killed, with many wounded. A *Leavenworth Conservative* correspondent waxed eloquent on the military prowess of these new additions to Union strength: "It is useless to talk any more about negro courage. The men fought like tigers, each and every one of them, and the main difficulty was to hold them well in hand. Saddle and mount are the word. These are the boys to clean out the bushwhackers."[146] According to Confederate leaders, "The Black devils fought like tigers… not one would surrender, though they had tried to take a prisoner."[147]

Next, this regiment of Black men defeated the Confederates at Honey Springs, Indian Territory. Not liking their defeat at the hands of Black soldiers, the Confederates were determined to get revenge for Honey Springs. That came on April 14, 1864, when the Confederate army met the 1st Kansas Colored Volunteers and two other regiments at Poison Springs, Arkansas. The battle was horrific. In celebrating their victorious revenge, Confederate soldiers took no Black prisoners—no mercy was given those who lay wounded on the battlefield. Many of these bodies were mutilated beyond recognition. The Clark brothers made no mention of these military actions, although Edward's medical records indicated damage to his right eye from gunpowder burns and a gunshot wound he sustained in 1864.

Confederate soldiers described what they witnessed at the incident at Poison Springs. Lieutenant William M. Stafford, a Texas artilleryman in Maxey's division, confided in his journal, "The surprise of the enemy was complete—at least 400 darkies were killed. [N]o black prisoners were captured." Another Arkansas cavalryman wrote, "If the negro was wounded our men would shoot him dead as they were passed and what negroes that were captured have…since been shot."[148]

Colonel James M. Williams, commander of the 1st Kansas (Colored), sent a field report to Major General Frederick Steele saying, "Many wounded men belonging to the First Kansas Colored Volunteers fell into the hands of the enemy, and I have the most positive assurances from eye-witnesses that they were murdered on the spot."[149]

David Clark

"I was born a slave of Link Robbeson....He joined the Rebel army before I enlisted."[150] While still in the service, David was admitted to the company hospital for one month. Medical personal sent him to St. Joseph's hospital for one month for the treatment of scurvy. David attributes his contracting scurvy "drinking cold swamp water in Little Rock, Arkansas."[151] In any event, the disease took its toll on his oral health. By the age of seventy-nine, he had lost all his teeth. His physician in 1895 stated, "I find all teeth have disappeared...gums have appearance of sponginess....I am of the opinion that owing to the scurvy and rheumatism that this man suffered from in the Army his health has been impaired."[152]

A deposition dated three years later by I.L. Eastman of Soda Springs, Bannock County, Idaho, was a witness to David's illness progression:

> During the year 1864—to the best of my knowledge and belief it was the month of October—he called at my drug store in Soda Springs, Idaho and was treated by Dr. J.W. Kirkwood for rheumatism, scurvy, and bronchitis. That he was quite lame from the disease...that I put up medicine for him that time and also several times during the years 1892–1893 and 1895.[153]

At the conclusion of David's enlistment and for the next fifty-six years, he traveled from Wyandotte to Seattle—stopping at some cities along the way and making a life for himself. In 1870, he moved from Kansas to Helena, Montana, where the occupation of ranching seemed to suit him. He purchased four hundred acres of land in Bonneville County, Idaho, between the years 1890 and 1908.[154] From 1875 to 1920, David spent most of his life working the land into a ranch and working in the quartz mines of Idaho. In Idaho, the effects of the Civil War started to affect his health and his ability to do manual labor.

On several occasions, David explained how the health issues of the Civil War had a lasting effect on him:

I was taken to the Camp Hospital remained there for weeks then taken to the general hospital in January 1865 at Little Rock Arkansas with scurry [unreadable] & an again at Co given medicine from the same remained there about one month & later in August 1865 & then the regiment moved to Pine Bluff & was unable any further duty in the army…also in Hospital at Mound city in Sept 7 Oct 1865.[155]

David applied to the Bureau of Pensions under the laws governing Civil War soldiers who were suffering from disabilities. His application in 1892 was granted, and he received his pension. He saw his pension increase to forty-five dollars per month by 1918. For the next few years, he underwent physical examinations and evaluations by government physicians in order to keep his monthly pension.[156] When David applied for another increase in his pension, his application was rejected. He had given the examiners three different birthdates and could not justify any of the dates. As a slave, his mother did not receive a birth certificate or even an entry in a family Bible.

By 1917, David's health had deteriorated to the point of requiring daily assistance of a caretaker. A decision was made for David to move to Seattle to be closer to his brother Edward and his family. Edward's daughter, Cora Clark Adams Grimes, became David's primary caretaker until his death. In a very short note, Cora communicated the death of her uncle to the Bureau of Pensions: "I now take these few spare moments to drop you these lines to say that my dear Uncle Mr. David Clark…passed away."

Part of David's estate was stocks in Radio Corporation of America (RCA). In an article dated 1964, his grandniece, Martha Anderson, filed suit in a Portland, Oregon court to recover the value of those stocks. However, the Court of San Francisco denied her claim.[157] Martha Anderson was the daughter of Cora Adams and granddaughter of David's brother Edward Clark. In addition, David had a ten-acre ranch with a value of $750 that he left to his brother Edward's daughters, Ethel Elegan and Cora Clark Adams Grimes. A Metropolitan Life Insurance policy was left to Edward.

David was single and left no descendants.

When David's grave was found in Lake View Cemetery, his grave marker, a small brick, was discovered beneath a very tall holly tree. On May 18, 2021, a modern Civil War gravestone was installed beside the smaller one, suggesting that David is buried under the tree. That new headstone was dedicated by the Sons of Union Veterans of the Civil War (SUVCW) on July 28, 2023.

Edward Clark

Unlike his brother, Edward found a different life's path. He returned to Wyandotte, Kansas, after his enlistment ended in 1865. He immediately found work as a farm laborer working alongside several of his brothers—David, Thomas and Alexander. All were working for Harry Harrison.

On May 10, 1868, Edward married the former Martha Jane Armstrong, daughter of Robert and Elizabeth Armstrong, in a ceremony officiated by Elder James Poke. While living in Kansas, they had three children before moving to Denver, Colorado. Martha and Edward had an additional four children before her death on October 9, 1897.

"Edward Clark, Civil War Veteran Answers Last Summons." From the *Northwest Enterprise. Courtesy of Library of Congress.*

Edward married again on May 10, 1916, to Francis Johnson. She filed for divorce after four years of marriage. Edward stated in his affidavit of October 12, 1920, "She sent me home on 20th of May 1916. I was no [ac]count so the judge gave her a divorce." The divorce was granted on September 14, 1918. There were no children born to this marriage.

Edward found employment in Denver working in a government building as a common laborer. In an accident, Edward injured himself pushing a wheelbarrow of concrete up an incline; he fell off the incline, injuring his side and causing a hernia. This was a major injury.

Like his brother David, Edward also applied for a pension as a former Civil War soldier on August 20, 1890. Government physicians subjected him to many physical examinations. It was during one of those examinations that the doctor noted "GSW in the stomach," which Edward stated he sustained in July 1864, and blindness in right eye due to powder burns during the same month.

After a few years living in Denver, Edward and several of his children moved to Seattle. The local Seattle newspaper interviewed Edward in connection with Lincoln's birthday celebration. The article described Edward's experience on the slave auction block, his running away and his joining the army to fight during the Civil War:[158]

Sixty-seven years ago, Edward Clark was auctioned off as a slave for $1,200. Then the Civil War broke out and Clark ran away to join the

Union Army when President Lincoln issued the emancipation proclamation. The only colored member of the G.A.R. in Washington, he is today helping celebrate the birthday of the Great Emancipator.[159]

Clark was one of many veterans who observed the day, recalling incidents of many years ago. At Veterans' Hall in the Armory, little groups fought it out all over again, this time minus the bitterness that marked the clash of 1862:[160]

Two years later, Edward appeared in another newspaper article. He had been in Olympia, Washington watching a parade of GAR members celebrating the golden anniversary encampment of the Grand Army. He retold his story with far more details than before. He was nineteen when sold from the auction block at Liberty, Missouri:

"In July 1861, his master, a Confederate quartermaster, took him up on the battle line to serve as cook and general flunky. At Christmas, Clark was sent home for a two-week's vacation....I'm still on that furlough."[161]

During that trip home, he crossed a frozen Missouri River:

[A]*lthough its banks were heavily guarded by rebels soldiers to prevent any negroes escaping, Clark slipped across and worked his way to Topeka, Kansas first as a rail-splitter; and then sold whiskey to the Indians. "I kept those Injuns drunk until July 5 of '62....When Abraham Lincoln issued that proclamation making us niggers into men I was given a regular standing in the army."*[162]

While Clark was still contraband, he and 23 other negros, under command of a [lieu]*tenant, were sent out to forage some food. They were getting corn from a large crib when they were surprised by guerrillas. Twenty-two of the group, including the lieutenant, were killed, and Clark escaped with his life by jumping across a ravine which four horses, ridden by the guerrillas, failed to jump. The horses and rebels were killed "and that's God's truth," the Grand Army man declared.*[163]

Clark came away from the war with a few souvenirs that included a coat, torn by bullets in six places, and a bullet in his stomach that was removed at some risk to his life. Edward remarked that he hoped he would live to see the next GAR encampment scheduled for September 1932 in Springfield, Illinois, but he died the following August.

Edward lived in Seattle until 1932, staying with his daughters Della Clark and Cora Clark Adams Grimes when his health issues became serious. His doctor immediately admitted him into the Naval Hospital in Bremerton, Washington, for evaluation and tests. The tests revealed that he had cancer, and it was spreading; the Naval Hospital was not equipped to treat the cancer. The hospital arranged to send him to the Veterans Hospital in Hines, Illinois, for treatment. He arrived there by train on August 8, 1932, for evaluation and treatment but died on August 11, 1932, before they started treatment.

An autopsy performed on Edward Clark found that cancer had spread to the spine and other parts of the body—the cancer had metastasized from the prostate.

His remains arrived by train at Seattle, where burial at the GAR Cemetery on Capitol Hill took place. He still has descendants living in the Seattle and Denver areas.[164]

JOHN H. DONEGAN

August 10, 1844–February 17, 1925
Huntsville, Madison County, Alabama—Seattle, King County, Washington
Mount Pleasant Cemetery
Seattle, King County, Washington
Private, Company Unassigned,
106th Regiment, United States Colored Infantry
September 2, 1864–May 1, 1865
Nashville, Tennessee—Jackson, Tennessee

John H. Donegan[165] was born into slavery to Hannah Donegan of Huntsville, Alabama, and owned by wealthy merchant James J. Donegan, an Irishman.[166]

This man became one of the many thousands of soldiers, both Black and white, captured by the Confederate army. While on garrison duty, this eighteen-year-old and 150 other members of the 106th were captured on September 24, 1864, at Athens, Alabama, by Major General Nathan Bedford Forrest's soldiers.

Prior to the assault, in a communication dated September 20, 1864, General Joseph Wheeler ordered, "The following troops of this corps will immediately report to Major General Forrest and accompany him on his expedition into Middle Tennessee: Colonel McLemore, with the 4th Tennessee, Colonel Nixon, with Nixon's Regiment and Colonel Biffie, commanding a brigade of Tennessee Troops." In obedience to this order, the regiment joined General Forrest in time to take part in the capture of Athens, Alabama, on September 24.[167]

Forrest, when negotiating with Colonel Campbell his surrender of the fort, stated, "Should you however, accept the terms, all white soldiers shall be treated as prisoners of war and the negroes returned to their masters."[168] At about nine o'clock, an unsigned demand for surrender was sent in under a flag of truce and was returned unanswered. A second demand signed "Major General Forrest" was refused. Forrest asked for a personal interview with Campbell, showed him that the Confederate force numbered eight to ten thousand men and again demanded the fort and its garrison surrender at noon.[169]

He later changed the terms of the surrender and allowed Campbell's commissioned officers to go to Mississippi to a facility under the control of the Confederate army. A regimental muster roster for the 110th U.S. Colored Infantry—it, too, was captured—indicated that the officers were sent to Mississippi and later exchanged for their Confederate counterparts in November 1864, while the captured enlisted men, including Black soldiers, were forced to march to Mobile, Alabama, to help in preparing the defenses of that city. The city fell on April 12, 1865.

An affidavit given by Private Joseph Howard of the 110th USCI stated:

I was taken prisoner at the surrender of Athens, Ala, Sept. 24, 1864. We were marched to Mobile, Ala., stopping at various places on the route. We were twelve days going to Mobile. After we were captured, the rebels robbed us of everything we had that they could use. They searched our pockets—took our clothing, and even cut the buttons off what little clothing they allowed us to retain. After arriving at Mobile, we were placed at work on the fortification there, and impressed colored men who were at work when we arrived, were released, we taking their places. We were kept at hard labor and inhumanly treated. If we lagged, or faltered, or misunderstood an order, we were whipped and abused—some of our own men being detailed to whip the others. They gave, as a reason for such harsh treatment, that we knew very well what they wanted us to do—but that we feigned ignorance—that if we were with the Yankees we would do all they want &c. For the slightest caused we were subjected to the lash. We were very poorly provided for with food, our rations being corn-meal and mule meat, and occasionally some poor beef.[170]

John did not discuss the incident in his pension records or mention that he spent his entire military service as a POW along with his brother Richard. He did mention treatment by an army surgeon in the prison hospital tent for overexposure in December 1864. A letter in John's pension file from the Chief, Record and Pension Office, makes clear his capture:

> *I am directed by the Secretary of War to inform you that it has been determined by this Department that this soldier was captured by the enemy at Athens, Alabama, September 24th, 1864, and held as a prisoner of war until on or about May 1, 1865, when he was released.*[171]

John and those in the 106th and 110th Regiments were transferred to Morgan's Castle prison and held there until May 1865. Conditions at the prison were not conducive to holding thousands of Union soldiers:

> *The Union prisoners endured these hardships with courage, but it was the flood during March of 1865 that broke the health of many. On March 1, 1865, the water runoff from the winter season caused the Alabama River to swell beyond its banks to the extent that it covered the entire prison floor. Of the 3,000 or so inmates, only about 600 found refuge from the chilly water by huddling together on rough banks called "roosts." The remaining 2,500 had no choice but to stand knee deep in the cold Alabama River. This deplorable condition lasted for 48 continuous hours during which the men could not build any fires with which to secure warmth or to cook their meager daily ration of course cornmeal. On the second day the camp commander issued crackers for the starving prisoners which did little to alleviate their suffering. Finally on the third day, cordwood was brought to the Union men which allowed them to build small platforms above the water upon which the exposed troops could crowd together to remove themselves from the icy water.*[172]

When John returned home after the end of the war, he applied for his pension. His original health declaration started on July 12, 1892, where he alleged "rheumatism disease of the heart." On March 28, 1907, in a statement of rejection, the examiner explained:

> *Rejection on the ground that the evidence does not show, and claimant has declared his inability to furnish proof that he's over sixty two years of age*

at date of exceeding the pending declaration, and he is not therefore, entitled to the benefits of the act of February 6, 1907.[173]

After his discharge from the service, John stayed in Tennessee for the next six or seven years. There he met and later married Julia McGuire on March 15, 1871. By 1873, the family were living in a small community just outside of Birmingham, Alabama. John and Julia had become the parents of seventeen children—only five to survive to adulthood.

John and his family had moved to Seattle, Washington, by 1908, by which time their grandson Jerry T. Donegan Jr. had also been born. After the death of John in February 1925, Julia Donegan attempted to get a tombstone for her husband. In a handwritten letter dated December 17, 1925, to the commissioner of pensions, Julie wrote:

> [John] *said Uncle Sam would take care of me. I thank Uncle Sam, oh what would I do if it were not for Uncle Same. I took good care of him. I loved him. He loved me. He was beared* [sic] *with miltry honors. I asked the department please give me a tombstone for my deceased Husband, John H. Donegan, please.*[174]

In response, the commissioner of pensions suggested that she needed to write to the Quartermaster General Office. There was no further communication between the parties, and there is no tombstone on his grave. A follow-up letter to the National Archives and Records Administration inquiring about Julia Donegan's application for a headstone for John was sent. Pertinent information about John was provided: full name, date of birth and death, service dates, regiment and company, as well as Julia's request expressed in her letter dated 1925. A response was received on May 16, 2022, giving an additional repository in St. Louis that would hold Julia's application.[175] An e-mail was received the next day with several online, searchable databases to use to locate Julia's application. A diligent effort to locate the application was made, to no avail.[176]

John is buried at Mount Pleasant Cemetery with his wife, Julia, son Jerry Thomas and the ashes of his daughter Billie Donegan Collins.

He has descendants living in the Seattle area.

GREEN FIELDS

August 4, 1836–August 1, 1914
Fayette County, Mississippi—Seattle, King County, Washington
Mount Pleasant Cemetery
Seattle, King County, Washington
Corporal, Company I, 2ⁿᵈ Regiment, U.S. Colored Light Artillery
December 23, 1864–December 22, 1865
St. Louis, Missouri—Memphis, Tennessee

Green was born to slave parents, Richard and Fannie Jackson Fields, while in the ownership of Alexander W. and Elizabeth Jane Fields. Green was the first in his family to volunteer to fight in the Civil War. He enrolled in St. Louis and was stationed at Camp Benton Barracks, just outside St. Louis, Missouri. He never saw any action on the battlefield.

Green was married to Martha Flynn in Memphis, Tennessee, on October 5, 1865, by the chaplain of the 11ᵗʰ U.S. Colored Infantry.[177] Martha brought into the family a little boy, Louis Hall, from an earlier slave relationship with Charles Hall; he was about two years old. Green was the only father Louis knew, and Louis assumed Green's surname.

The family remained in Missouri for many years after the war. Louis remained in St. Louis when Green and Martha moved to Seattle in 1893. They lived at several addresses in Seattle: 2713 4ᵗʰ Street, 213 4ᵗʰ Avenue North and, finally, 1924 1ˢᵗ Avenue West.

Louis married Della E. Scott of Missouri in about 1885. They both resided there until their deaths in 1917 and 1949, respectively. There were no children born to this couple. They maintained their residence at 6109 Broadway Street, St. Louis, Missouri (that home is no longer standing).

Green was well known in the Queen Anne community. On one occasion, he was photographed while raking in front of his home. Many a resident remarked on his willingness to work hard. A painting of the photograph was submitted to the Paris Exposition and was a prizewinner.

For a long time, Green was a worker for the City of Seattle, even though he suffered with a disability from the effects of the war. At his initial medical examination in January 1892, he told the physicians that in the winter of 1865, while on guard duty at the time, he experienced frostbite of the toes. This was confirmed at the time of examination. The doctors noted that the big toes on both feet were contracted from frostbite. He also said that he had rheumatism especially during the winter months.

Green Fields,
Civil War soldier.
From the *Seattle
Republican. Courtesy
of Library of
Congress.*

After several more examinations, rejections and re-applications, he was approved in February 1908, with his first pension check for two months delivered in June.

With the help of the late Loretta Edwards of Mount Pleasant Cemetery, an application for a headstone for Green Fields was sent to the Department of Veterans Affairs in June 2007; the headstone was acquired and installed. His grave site is now part of the Queen Anne Historical Society's tour in the months of June/July, and he is one of four African American Civil War soldiers identified in that cemetery: Henry Carper, John Donegan, Green Fields and George Rawles.

There are no living descendants of Green Fields.

CLARK E. HARRIS

December 25, 1849–July 22, 1911
Covington, Newton County, Georgia—Issaquah, King County, Washington
Hillside Cemetery
Issaquah, King County, Washington
Private, Company B, 15th United States Colored Infantry
October 20, 1864–April 7, 1866
Springfield, Tennessee—Nashville, Tennessee

Born in Covington, Newton County, Georgia, Clark Harris was the child of Clara Cunningham Harris along with brothers Charles, George and Joseph and an unidentified sister. A wealthy merchant turned farmer, state senator and then judge, John Harris, and his wife, Susan Ann, of the same county, owned the family.

At the age of fourteen, Clark ran away from this owner to join the Union army in Tennessee. He enlisted as a steward but later was assigned the rank of drummer in Company B of the 15th Regiment of the U.S. Colored Infantry for three years and was due a bounty of $300. When he enlisted, he measured five feet, three inches tall and had black eyes and hair and a yellow complexion. He had no battle experience. The regiment remained close to the post at Springfield, Tennessee.

On October 20, 1865, some members of the 15th Regiment were stationed at Springfield, Tennessee's penitentiary, standing guard during the execution of Samuel Champ Ferguson, a notorious Confederate guerrilla, who had been recently judged and rendered guilty in the killing of Union soldiers both Black and white at Saltville, Virginia. The watchers of the hanging were very uncomfortable with "colored" soldiers standing guard.[178]

After mustering out of the army, Clark went to Iowa and stayed with his former commanding officer until January 1867, when the work of steam boater lured him to the Mississippi River. In St. Paul on October 1, 1869, he enlisted into the U.S. Army Cavalry but became a deserter the next month. There was no reason given for his desertion.

For the next six or seven years, Clark worked his way up and down the Mississippi River on the *War Eagle* and *Damsel*, stopping at ports in New Orleans, Memphis, St. Louis and St. Paul.[179] He spent two years living in Mississippi before moving on to Missouri, where he met his first wife, Maud Susan Graves Webb. Called "Suzie" by her family, she was born in Pike County, Missouri, in 1855 to Lewis and Emma Gray/Graves. She was part

Left: Maud Harris, daughter of Clark Harris and his first wife, Maud Susan Harris. *Photo in possession of Peter Gamble.*

Right: Elizabeth Felstead Harris, second wife of Clark Harris. *Photo in possession of Donna Kennedy.*

of a family that included two sisters and one brother: Jane, Lucy and Green. Maud met Clark in Clarksville, Missouri, where she worked for a local family as a domestic. She had previously married Zachariah Webb in February 1871; he died sometime during the year 1876. Their only child, Willie, died early in his life.

Sometime prior to Zach Webb's death, Clark and Maud moved to La Crosse, Wisconsin, where they had five children: J. Josephine, Clark M., Maud, Walter C. and Louis Harris. A sixth child, Ross, born to Maud later in her life, was not the son of Clark.[180] After the birth of Louis, difficulties in the relationship caused Clark and Maud to separate; Clark moved to St. Paul, Minnesota.

The pension board examiners tried to determine when Maud applied for a divorce from Zach; they questioned many of Zach and Maud's family, but no information was found. There was much discussion as to whether Maud and Clark ever married. Several said yes but could not recall the date or place. Maud's half-sister, Eliza Graves Wilcox, claimed that she had been invited to a small ceremony performed by Pastor Cheers, but she did not attend the wedding. A search of several county records by the examiner turned up nothing to confirm the marriage of Clark to Maud. They lived openly as husband and wife, even calling each other such around their friends and family.

In St. Paul, Clark found employment with the Salvation Army. It was there he met a very young Elizabeth Felstead, daughter of William and Elizabeth Felstead. Elizabeth was born in 1873 in Ontario, Canada. The Felsteads immigrated to the United States in about 1860 but crossed the Canadian border many times. Elizabeth's sister, Rebecca, was born in New York. This family stayed on the move but eventually found a home in Michigan and Minnesota for some years.

It took him six years before he approached her with an offer of marriage. In Clark's pension file, a deposition from Elizabeth's father stated that he was not very happy with the idea of his daughter marrying a "colored man," even though at the time Minnesota laws did not forbid interracial marriages. She married Clark on November 23, 1892, despite her father's objections and without evidence that Clark had divorced his first wife, Maud.

On December 2, 1892, an enraged William went to the St. Paul legal system and asked to have Clark arrested for bigamy and thrown into jail. With legal documents in place, Clark's first wife was asked to come to St. Paul from La Crosse to testify. She went even though she was suffering from the effects of measles. She acknowledged that she married Clark and even pointed him out in the court. The attorney for Clark objected. According to the laws of Minnesota, a wife cannot testify against her husband without his permission—something Clark refused to give. The court decided that since Maud was the only witness against Clark, she could not testify and therefore he would not be charged with bigamy; he was released from incarceration:

> *Judge Otis has ordered Clark Harris discharged from the custody of the sheriff. Harris was held to the grand jury by the municipal court on a charge of bigamy. C. Tyson Butcher applied for his discharge on a writ of habeas corpus....Judge Otis holds that the evidence on which Harris was held was insufficient and, does not justify such committal to jail.*[181]

Maud went back home and died fifteen years later on September 28, 1907, after an illness of a year from dropsy.[182]

This was not the only time Clark skirted the law. In January 1892, he became involved with a white woman named Maria Zell who worked at the same Salvation Army as Clark. Marriage between the two was agreed to before Clark suspected that Maria was seeing another man. When he refused to marry her, she had him arrested "on a charge of assault and battery and threatening to kill her…he had assaulted her and he had menaced her with a razor."[183] The judge was not impressed with the case and "discharged the defendant."

Clark and Elizabeth stayed in St. Paul for the next four or five years and became the parents of three children: David, Effie and Elizabeth. The decision to move the family was a major one. The quest for a better life led the family to Washington State, specifically Seattle, in 1899. Here they had ten additional children; of the ten, three died between 1898 and 1909. The last child, Andrew, was born the year following Clark's death. The children who survived to adulthood were Ruth, Grace, Dorothy, Edward, Clarence and Ralph; children who did not included Jennie, Carroline and Rebecka (the spelling in later documents was "Rebecca"). The family lived in the Seattle area until November 1910. Clark and his wife had the opportunity to purchase a farm of forty acres in the Upper Valley of Issaquah, Washington; they assumed the current mortgage of $2,500. The farm was a place where the children had a chance to grow up strong and healthy while he worked to sustain a living as a painter, plasterer and farmer. The dream was short-lived. Clark died suddenly on July 22, 1911, of peritonitis, brought on by organic heart disease.

A ceremony by the members Prilliman and Goode of the Grand Army of the Republic (GAR) Post buried Clark at Hillside Cemetery in Issaquah, Washington.

Right after Clark's death, his wife hired Andrew R. Black[184] as her advocate to assist her in the process of obtaining her widow's pension. Andrew started a letter writing campaign on behalf of Elizabeth Harris. He informed the pension board:

> *I am attending to the widow's affairs and if additional affidavits or other matters require attention and are necessary I will thank you to communicate with me direct. I believe the widow is entitled to the pension of Harris from June 4th 1911 to the time of his death, July 22, 1911.*[185]
>
> *It will be noted that Mr. Harris died July 22nd, 1911, I am of the opinion that the widow is entitled to the accrued pension for the time pensioner was alive. If this is according to law I will thank you to forward*

to my address the blanks and information as to the procedure necessary to establish the fact that the widow is entitled to this pension.[186]

In the light of the receipt of your communication referred to in the 1st paragraph hereof, if not inconsistent with the rules of your office, will you kindly acknowledge the receipt of the declarations in question and advise if anything whatever can be done to expedite matters in any form or manner.[187]

A search is being made in Minnesota for a relative who can make such an affidavit, and if found, same will be forwarded later. You must realize that such a requirement is an exceedingly difficult one, particularly in this section of the country where the population is constantly moving about and conditions generally were not settled as far back as 1892.[188]

Will you kindly advise me at your earliest convenience as to the present status of the case, and when we are likely to obtain final decision in the matter?[189]

...please find herewith enclosed special power attorney from Mrs. Elizabeth Harris to me. This, I believe will meet your requirements in order that subsequent information and communications may be forwarded to me direct, thereby saving considerable time in attending to the matters required by the Department.

You are also advised that as the records of this Bureau do not show that you have been admitted to practice before it under the provisions of the act of July 4, 1884, you cannot be recognized as attorney in any claim pending before the Bureau. The necessary instructions to enable you to apply for admission to practice before this Bureau are herewith enclosed.[190]

Opposite: Home of the family of Clark Harris at 305 West Highway, Issaquah, Washington. Photo dated 1940. *Courtesy of Puget Sound Archives, Bellevue, Washington.*

Above: Death certificate for Clark Harris. *Author's collection.*

Clark left behind nine children, a pregnant wife and a farm with mortgages and other debts. Elizabeth struggled to keep the ranch by selling eggs and butter, but the expenses were overwhelming. The local lending institutions refused to help. Within Clark's probate records,[191] two individuals were identified as holding mortgages on the property: C.E. Owens (first mortgage with interest $2,900) and E.F.B. Richardson (second mortgage with interest $705). Once the probate of Clark's estate was complete, Elizabeth was left with nothing; her lawyer, Andrew Black, took the last $25 as his fee. Elizabeth was forced to move herself and her children to the Greenwood neighborhood in Seattle, where her parents lived. She took a job as a grocery clerk to support her family.

As a widow of a Civil War soldier, she thought that she was entitled to Clark's pension of twelve dollars per month and two dollars per month per minor child living in the household. Elizabeth applied on August 19, 1911, for Clark's pension as her right of a widow. There were searches by the pension board examiner to find individuals who were familiar with the family's history and current situation, including soliciting information from several children of his first wife: Josephine, Walter C. and Maude S. Harris. The examiner found several men who reportedly worked with Clark on the Mississippi River.

The witnesses testified about the situation regarding the first marriage of Clark Harris to Maud Susan, and the witnesses acknowledged that they suspected that his second wife, Elizabeth, knew that Clark had been married and that there had not been a divorce from the first wife. The examiner asked Elizabeth to produce proof that her husband had been divorced from Maud Susan before she could be accepted as the legal wife of Clark. The problem encountered by Elizabeth was that Maud Susan was now dead. Maud's older children testified that they knew of no effort of their mother to secure a divorce from Clark. In fact, her son Walter stated, "[I]f she had not died so early, his mother would have applied for the pension."

In October 1913, Elizabeth received a letter from the pension board rejecting her application for Clark's pension because her marriage was not legal and the State of Washington did not acknowledge common-law marriages. This was heartbreaking information. Subsequent letters written on her behalf requested another look at her application. Again, the pension board referred her to the letter of 1913 as a reason for the rejection.

Her children grew up and slowly moved out of Seattle. The eldest son, David, moved to Montana but returned to Seattle in 1931 to aid the family with burial of Elizabeth's father. William and Elizabeth Felstead had previously moved to Seattle to help their son-in-law William Fisler with raising his three children after the death of Elizabeth's sister Rebecca Fisler. William and Elizabeth Felstead died on March 1, 1931, and April 1, 1926, respectively; both are buried at Crown Hill Cemetery in the center of the Greenwood neighborhood.

Elizabeth Harris lived until 1956, when she succumbed to a cerebral incident. She, too, is buried at Crown Hill Cemetery.

While researching Clark Harris, a family member was found from the second family on Ancestry.com. Donna Kennedy of California was at once contacted. She helped fill in some of the missing information with some of the family's oral history and provided pictures of Clark and Elizabeth's children.

An effort was successfull in finding a descendant from Clark's first marriage.

Clark's only surviving granddaughter, Gladys, is 103 years old.[192]

Clark has descendants in California, Minnesota, Oregon and Wisconsin.

GILFORD PETER HERVEY

June 9, 1842–September 8, 1920
Halifax County, North Carolina—Sedro-Woolley, Skagit County, Washington
Grand Army of the Republic Cemetery
Seattle, King County, Washington
Private, Company F, 59th Regiment, United States Colored Infantry
(formerly 1st Tennessee African Descent)
June 10, 1863–January 32, 1866
LaGrange, Tennessee—Memphis, Tennessee

Gideon P. Harvey, the elder son of Peyton Pritchett, owned Gilford; his parents, Carey and Rosetta; and his siblings. This slave owner lived in Halifax County, North Carolina, before moving to Yalobusha County, Mississippi, around the summer of 1848 to work 482 acres of land he purchased.[193] Gilford was just a child when the move took place.

When Gilford joined the army, his and his comrades' clothing were more or less rags:

> *When this new regiment was formed, an officer described the moment the new recruits dressed in their new uniforms. The commander of the 59th*

U.S. Colored Infantry described the induction process for freedmen. The men stripped off their old clothes, tossed them into a fire, and stepped into a bath. Then they buttoned up their new blue coats, and the metamorphosis was complete. The office enthused, "Yesterday a filthy repulsive 'nigger,' today a neatly attired man; yesterday a slave, to-day a freeman; yesterday a civilian, today a soldier." [194]

Gilford and his comrades in arms were assigned to guard and fatigue duty at La Grange, Tennessee. On June 10, 1864, they along with the 55th U.S. Colored Infantry met Confederate major general Nathan Bedford Forrest on the battlefield of Brice's Cross Roads at Baldwyn, Mississippi. This brigade of soldiers helped Major General Samuel Davis Sturgis avoid capture by Forrest. Major E.H. Hanson reported:

All through the night the beaten army kept on their way, reaching Ripley, twenty-two miles from the battlefield, on the morning of July 11th. During the retreat the enemy captured fourteen pieces of artillery, our entire train of two hundred fifty wagons loaded with ammunition and ten days' rations. [195]

After mustering out, Gilford moved to Cairo, Illinois, to work. Gilford mentioned Gideon in his Civil War pension records: "A man named Gibbs or Gidd Hervey was my old master. He is dead. Benj & Jas Hervey his two sons were living near Water Valley in 1870 when my master left there and came to me in Cairo Ills. I have not heard from the boys since." [196] He stated in his deposition of January 29, 1896, "When I was mustered out of the service I was not well but came directly to Cairo, Ills & a little eating house & kept boarders on the corner of Walnut & 13th Sts for the steamboat boys."

He left there in 1870, moved to Cincinnati, Ohio, and opened up the same type of business in the West Walnut Hills. After several more moves back and forth between Illinois and Ohio, he moved to Larned, Kansas, and obtained eighty acres of land in 1889 through the Homestead Act of 1862, five miles east of Larned. [197] While living in Larned, Gilford started the process of applying for his Civil War pension on April 2, 1888. A physical examination by three physicians was required. He complained that while in La Grange, Tennessee, he was exposed to

measles, resulting in bronchitis and chronic diarrhea...August 1863; also mumps at Fort Pickens, Tennessee [date not stated]. *His treatment for that exposure according him was, "In Field Hospital at LaGrange about*

3 months—in field Hospl at Ft. Pickens about three months, for mumps, chronic diarrhea and bronchitis, about May 1, 1864."[198]

Eleven years later, his attorney received a response to his appeal of Hervey's rejection from the commissioner of pensions; Gilford had moved from Kansas to Indiana and then to California at the time he received the information. He claimed that he was entitled to an increase in his pension. After special examination, the claim was rejected by the bureau on March 14, 1899, on the grounds of no record of the disabilities alleged and of the claimant's inability, after special examination, to furnish satisfactory testimony to show their origin in the service. His muster roll for the years in the service showed that he was present on those months he claimed to have been hospitalized.

After reapplying and undergoing medical examinations several more times and one more rejection, he was finally approved and received the first increase in his check for the fourth quarter of 1907, while he was living in California.

Gilford's marital status changed many times over his lifetime. He married five times: Francis McLinn in Memphis (1864), Matilda Wethers in Illinois (1867), Annie Rankins in Illinois (1880, divorced in 1890), Mary E. Moss in Indiana (1893, divorced before 1900) and Naomi R. Russell in California (1902, divorced in 1914). He was the father of one child, a son, Carey Fleetwood Hervey, by wife number two. Mrs. (Eleanor) J.H. Whittler, who identified herself as his daughter, hired an attorney to locate Gilford.[199]

During his many years of travel, Gilford's main occupation aside from some light manual labor jobs was his ministry of the gospel. While living in Indiana in 1895, he was selected as pastor of a new church, the Free Independent Baptist Church of North Indianapolis. The congregation consisted of ten members.[200]

In 1909, Gilford worked with the community of North Yakima, Washington, to set up a new colony for African Americans. The parishioners of his church, Second Baptist Church, had purchased four tracts of land. The new colony hoped to build a new church on the same land. Gilford stated that because he had done so much traveling and had a large number of friends in the East, he could expand the church membership. "He believed that the type of citizens he is influencing to come to North Yakima will be a credit to the community and that they will do their share, in bettering themselves, toward building up a fine nation in this part of the union."[201]

While living in Yakima, Gilford paid for a newspaper ad saying that he wanted his wife, Naomi, to know about his feelings for her. This couple moved to Pasadena, California, in about 1913, where he worked as a grocer for a few years. After Naomi's divorce from Hervey, he moved to Seattle.

By early 1920, Hervey's mental state was deteriorating. He was committed to the Sedro Woolley Insane Asylum, Washington (today known as Northern State Mental Hospital), on August 26, 1920, for treatment of senile dementia.[202] A single statement on a "Petition for Letters of Administration" dated September 13, 1920, clarified his admission to the asylum: "The deceased was adjudged insane by the above entitled court [Superior Court of the State of Washington for the County of King], August 26, 1920, and sent to the Northern Hospital for Insane at Sedro Woolley aforesaid."[203]

On October 15, 1920, Gilford's only son, Carey, was notified of his father's death—presumably by the administrator of the asylum. Carey wrote to the commission of pensions:

> Will you please inform me whether or not the Pension check for Sept 1920 was sent to the late G.P. Hervey…whose address was Sta W. Box 843 Seattle Wash. If so who signed for him as he was at Sedro Woolley Hospital for Insane at the time…and [I] received no notice his being in the Asylum until he was dead and buried a month later.[204]

Carey lost contact with his father and attempted to contact him through a newspaper ad in a D.C. paper, the *National Tribune*, dated May 6, 1909.

Two years later, Carey wrote to the Department of the Interior to complain that there was something amiss with his father's estate. He had taken a trip to Washington and talked with his father's estate administrator, A.P. Lawrence:

> He failed to give in the entire estate & I made a trip out there July 1921 which lasted 2 mo's, paid off the Administrator & the Court awarded me the entire estate Oct 25th, 1921.…When I got to Seattle I found that all the personal property of any value had been destroyed; the chief things were $5000.00 in U.S. Gov bond bo[ugh]t some time in 1904 or 5 while father lived in Ohio. I have a "key" that was in a Grip satchel among deeds & paper turned over to me by administrator when he was paid off, however I didn't discover the key til I was back in Ohio.…Wrote back to Seattle to my attorneys, who said there is no such company there a year ago and there it rests.…I came to this city to see about a mortgage father held on real-estate & found the statues of Lim'd be 20 years and that the mortgage should have been foreclosed while in the Administrator's hand before Feb 2nd 1921. Sad lose over $2000 here on this.[205]

In reply to Cary's letter of September 5, 1922, he was told that any monies received by his father after his death became part of his estate and that "this bureau has no control whatever in the disposition of such moneys." They also suggested that he communicate with the "Treasury relative to the government bonds." Little did he know that the post office had returned the $161 check because someone wrote, "He was deceased."[206]

On October 1923, Carey wrote a letter to the pension commissioner again to let him know that as far as he knew, the last pension check for his father was not in his possession and that Mr. A.P. Lawrence of the GAR Post had returned the check. He also stated that he assumed that his stepmother had destroyed all his letters to his father, which was why he never returned Carey's letters. What Carey did not know was that they had divorced in 1914 and that his father had been living alone since then.

The Superior Court on October 25, 1921, had distributed Gilford's estate to the one and only heir, Carey; therefore any pension money was part of the estate. The pension check was issued on September 4, and his father died on September 8; it should have been part of the estate. There were no further communications from either party.

Jacqueline A.E. Lawson and Cynthia A. Wilson—Gilford Hervery discovery. Photo from March 5, 2004. *Courtesy of Museum of History and Industry's Photo Archives.*

In the many letters Carey sent inquiring about his father's location and his assets, he never mentioned that he was married or that he had children, and there's a good chance that Gilford had no idea he had grandchildren. Carey married nineteen-year-old Eura Johnson. The couple had three sons: Gilford Delaney (1903–1973), David Theodore (1905–1963) and Paul Dunbar (1913–1973). Paul was the only son who did not marry; the other sons had no children of their own.

The Black Genealogy Research Group of Seattle (BGRG) and the Church of Latter-day Saints (LDS) scheduled a Family History Summit on March 6, 2004. As part of the advance publicity, two members were interviewed about what the group did and some of the members' research projects. The subject of this soldier came up. The interviewees told the interviewer, John Iwasaki of the *Post-Intelligencer*, the story of Gilford Hervey and the eventual ancestral connection of Gilford to the Harvey family of Seattle through Colonel Thomas Hervey Sr. and his grandson Gideon T. Hervey.[207]

There are no living descendants of Gilford Hervey.

PIERCE COUNTY

JOHN H. CHRISTOPHER

December 23, 1842–March 1, 1908
Jacksonville, Duval County, Florida—Orting, Pierce County, Washington
Old Soldiers Home Cemetery
Orting, Pierce County, Washington
Private, Company D, 2nd South Carolina Colored Infantry
Private, Company D, 34th Regiment, United States Colored Infantry
May 22, 1863–February 29, 1864
Beaufort, South Carolina—Hilton Head, South Carolina

John spent ten months in the service before he was "discharged by order of Major General Gilmore." The records showed that he left because of the illness of his mother.

The limitation of information in his pension file made researching his history a little difficult. There were only thirty-four pages in the file. An effort to locate him in any census was thwarted either by the spelling of his name or by not finding him where he stated he was during the years after leaving the service of the infantry—in South Carolina, Oregon, California and British Columbia.

John stated in one of the records that he was living in Victoria, British Columbia, from 1868 through 1871. A search of the city directory for that city found nothing. Using city directories for Portland, Oregon, and Seattle/

Tacoma, Washington, John was immediately found. The Portland-area city directory had him living there between the years 1872 and 1895.[208] He was found working as a "jobber" and a bartender/porter in the National Hotel and residing at the American Exchange rooming house. In 1882, John worked and resided in the Occidental Hotel. An entry in the 1895 Portland City Directory listed him working at the Massasoit Hotel as a porter.

In the local newspaper, the *Oregonian Times*, an article dated 1873 indicated that John had gone to court and had a case against A. Carr. That court case found for the defendant, Carr, and ordered John to pay one dollar in damages.[209]

He resided in the city of Tacoma, Washington, from 1893 through 1897 at the Massasoit Hotel, where he worked.

Between 1898 and 1905, John was living in Seattle and working as a porter. When he started to feel the effects of the war, he applied for residence at the Soldiers Home at Orting Washington, where he was admitted for "partial disability from rheumatism and old age….He is suffering from rheumatism and enlarged prostate."[210] He died there in 1908 and is buried at its cemetery.

He was single, with no apparent descendants. He stated that his next of kin was Mrs. Charles Scott of Alaska and Mrs. Lathrop of British Columbia. Their relationships to Christopher have not been established.

AUGUSTUS M. DIXON

1846–September 13, 1911
Sumter County, Alabama—Orting, Pierce County, Washington
Old Soldiers Home Cemetery
Orting, Pierce County, Washington
Private, Company E, 60th Regiment, United States Colored Infantry
January 19, 1864–October 15, 1865
Burlington, Iowa—Devall's Bluff, Arkansas

Augustus was born and raised in Greene County, Alabama, and owned by Joseph Arrington Sr. When Arrington's son, Edward, enlisted in the Confederate army, he was given Augustus as his personal body servant. It was at the Battle of Corinth, Mississippi (October 3–4, 1862), that his master lost sight of fifteen-year-old Augustus. Later found by Union officer George Burnett of the 7th Iowa Infantry, Augustus was taken to Iowa:

Was out there [Iowa] *about two years, I guess and then enlisted at Burlington, Iowa was mustered in at Helena, Ark in January 1865 and M/O at Duvalls Bluff, Ark in October 1865. My father was named Dick Arrington and when I got away from slavery and from my master I was advised to change my name. So I took the name of Dixon. Was never known by name of Dixon before I went to Iowa.*[211]

In an episode of *Finding Your Roots*, Dr. Louis Gates introduced Pharrell Williams to his ancestor Jane Arrington, who was interviewed by the WPA for *Slave Narratives*. Dixon and his family were owned by a set of Arringtons who were probably related to Jane's owners.[212]

Even though he says that he did not use any other name, he frequently referred to his usage of "May" (his middle name) as a surname. In fact, when he married Lizzie Todd, he used the surname of "May." His son George used "May" as his surname and "Dixon" as his middle name.

At the time of his entering the army, he joined as a substitute for G. Scott McDonald Walnut of Marshall County, Iowa. Under this agreement, the individual who is substituting is given $300 for his service, and the other individual is free to go home and live as he sees fit. So, Augustus was assigned to Company A of the 60th U.S. Colored Infantry.

According to statements made in his pension file, Augustus May Dixon spent several months in Galesburg, Knox County, Illinois, during the years of 1869 and 1870, teaching at one of the local colored schools.[213] There was a school only a few blocks from where he was living in the boardinghouse of Melissa Alexander on Broad Street. A document was located in the Knox College Library: "Blacks in Galesburg: City Directory Information."[214] It listed Blacks living in Galesburg for the years 1857, 1861 and 1867, and it did not include Dixon. In 1867, he went back to Oskaloosa, Iowa, and was there about one year, spending part of that time in the "Quaker School." Augustus May moved to Galesburg, Illinois, in 1869 to further his education.

By the summer of 1870, Augustus May (now using the name Gus May) was living in the small town of Grinnell, Iowa. He no longer taught school but rather applied his trade of choice: barbering. H.D. Works, a hotel keeper, employed him, and he resided in the same hotel.

On the move again, Augustus was teaching in the small town of Rutherford, Missouri, working for the public school system managed by Superintendent A.B. Campbell during the years 1872 through 1875.

Yearning to be a barber again, Augustus traveled throughout the state of Nebraska during the years of 1875 through 1886.[215] Those years were the worst for him. He was battling with the pension board to get a pension commensurate with his health issues. The board seemed to think that his health issues were not the result of the Civil War. Augustus was required to find friends, doctors or anyone to vouch for his health issues.

His pension file had several affidavits from individuals who could attest to his inability to do manual labor, problems with his eyes and the likelihood that smallpox and mumps exacerbated his health problems.

Augustus initially applied for his pension under the Law of 1862 and received a letter of rejection. He applied again under the Law of 1890 and received a pension of twelve dollars per month. However, this was not enough, and he wanted more; he thought that contracting mumps and smallpox during the war entitled him to additional funds. Special examiners interviewed those individuals who knew him to get their opinion of Augustus's health issues. The examiner was tasked to determine if those individuals were "believable." The examiner then wrote reports to the pension board with their opinion. Augustus appealed the "dismissed" decisions. It was not until 1898 that Augustus's attorney, R.A. Crossman, submitted a "Brief and Argument" to the commissioner of pensions. In the brief, the attorney argued that the examiner was biased against his client:

> We desire in conclusion to call attention to the fact that in this case it seems from all the information we can gather on the subject, that the special examination has in this case was conducted as a defense to this claim rather than as an aid. If your information in this be true, then we feel that we would be recreant to the trust imposed on us as the agent for the claimant did, we not call attention thereto and enter our protest again such special examination.[216]

Once the case was over, Augustus wrote two letters to the pension board complaining about how he was treated by two of the special examiners. They had suggested that he lied. Augustus barked back that he "never lies." Again, his application was rejected because he was not of sufficient age to receive an increase; a veteran had to be seventy years old—Augustus was fifty-two.

Augustus, now living in North Yakima, Washington, asked several residents of that town to vouch for his assertions. He asked William Phillips to do an affidavit to help him pursue an increase in his pension. He agreed and said:

> I met Augustus M. Dixon on May 14th, 1903, for the first time since leaving Duvall Bluff, Arkansas, thirty-eight years ago, and I cannot swear

positively that he is the identical individual referred to herein as having the mumps, to the best of my knowledge and belief, he is the man.[217]

Belle Evans, wife of Civil War soldier Jasper Evans, was the caretaker for Phillips. She, in a sworn deposition on February 13, 1907, stated,

[S]*he knows that said Dixon has frequently applied to the said Phillips, before his death, asking him to make an affidavit showing that he, Phillips, was acquainted with said Dixon during the said time of the Rebellion, and that said Dixon served in the same regiment as he did.*[218]

In conversations between Dixon and Phillips, "[S]he [Belle] heard said Phillips admitted remembering said Dixon as a member of said Regiment, and that the only reason that he gave or would ever give for refusing to sign the affidavit requested of him was that if he, the said Dixon was successful in his application for a pension, he would receive such a large sum of money as back pension that, the said Phillips, believed that it would be to said Dixon's detriment."[219]

Augustus never did get the increase in his pension. He was paid twenty-four dollars starting the first quarter of 1911, and his last payment was eight dollars on September 13, 1911.[220]

On August 31, 1911, while still a resident of North Yakima County and having his health deteriorate to the point of helplessness, Augustus applied for admission to the Soldiers Home in Orting, Washington. He was admitted on September 3, 1911; he died on September 13, 1911, at 2:00 a.m. and is now buried at the Washington Soldiers Home cemetery in Orting.

Augustus May Dixon left no surviving descendants in Washington but may have some in California and Oklahoma.

COLUMBUS HOLLINS

March 1, 1844–August 27, 1919
Charleston, Tallahatchie County, Mississippi—Washington State Soldiers Home
Soldiers Home Cemetery
Orting, Pierce County, Washington
Private, 1ˢᵗ Independent Battery, Minnesota Light Artillery
September 28, 1864–July 1, 1865

Vicksburg, Mississippi—St. Paul, Minnesota
Troop A, 10th United States Cavalry
November 1, 1869–December 29, 1874
St. Paul, Minnesota—Fort Griffin, Texas

Born to Jack Hollins and an enslaved woman, Columbus spent his early life as a cook's apprentice on two steamers, *War Eagle* and the *Belle of Memphis*, between the years 1850 and 1860. His deposition taken on May 26, 1914, in Pierce County, Washington, stated, "In the year 1850 affiant [he] was an apprentice learning the trade of a cook on a steamboat *War Eagle* and *Belle of Memphis* on the Mississippi River from New Orleans to St. Louis until 1860."[221]

Sometime between 1860 and 1863, Columbus got away from his owner and found his way to a camp of Union soldiers near Vicksburg, Mississippi. According to the muster roll for the Minnesota Light Artillery, he joined as "contra-band" and enlisted as an undercook on June 1863, according to General Order 323 of the War Department:[222]

> [T]*he two undercooks will be enlisted…on their enlistment papers showing that they are undercooks of African descent.…They will also be discharged in the same manner as other soldiers.*

Hollins talked little of his experiences during the war. He attributed his health issues to being constantly wet in Atlanta, where it seems he spent most of the last months of the war. He claimed that a "gun burst" contributed to his partial blindness while in Atlanta during Sherman's March to the Sea.

Company A's Lieutenant Henry S. Hurter, in his *Narrative of the First Battery of Light Artillery*, tells of several incidents included in their March to the Sea:

> *The next day* [November 8th] *Uncle Sam gladdened our hearts by paying us for eight months' service. After destroying the railroad leading north, all property either unserviceable or superfluous, we broke camp on November 13th, commencing our march to the sea.*[223]

Columbus spent the next four years living in St. Paul before joining Troop A of the U.S. 10th Regular Cavalry in that city. His service during the years 1869 through 1874 was under the command of Captain Nicholas Nolan and Lieutenants G. Fred Coake and Henry S. Hurter of Company A of the 10th Cavalry. He was one of two horse ferriers for the company.

Civil War field kitchen.
Courtesy of Library of Congress.

Within the monthly organization return, it listed Hollins as joining the 10th Cavalry in January 1870.[224]

Between 1867 and 1886, the 10th was engaged in extended campaigns against the Cheyennes, Kiowas, Comanches and Apaches in Kansas, New Mexico, Arizona and the Indian Territory. According to Benjamin H. Grierson, colonel of the 10th Cavalry from 1867 to 1890, the 10th acquired the name "Buffalo Soldiers" during the 1871 campaign against the Comanches in the Indian Territory. Grierson said that the Comanches respected the soldiers' tireless marching and dogged trail skills. They had earned the name of the rugged and revered buffalo. The 10th made the "Buffalo" its regimental coat of arms years later, but the term "Buffalo Soldiers" became synonymous with both the 9th and 10th units.[225]

For the next thirty years, Columbus traveled to cities over the western half of the United States—Denver, Salt Lake City, Butte and Portland—all the while working as a cook, in either restaurants or hotels. By the time he reached Tacoma, Washington, the ill effects of his service in the Civil War and his time in the U.S. Cavalry were starting to interfere with his ability to work as a cook.

When he applied for a pension, a physical examination was mandatory to prove that he had service-connected problems with his health. He was also required to provide proof of his birth, which was difficult for soldiers since birth certificates were not usually issued for slaves.

The physicians' examinations confirmed the many complaints Hollins expressed. He had vision problems in the left eye that resulted from "gun burst" when he was in Atlanta from September 7 through November 16, 1864; this was during the time of William T. Sherman's taking of Atlanta.

He also complained of rheumatism from lying on the damp ground during the same period. He wore glasses to help with his vision problem.

The physicians also noticed some tenderness of the testicles and enlargement of the prostate that Hollins associated with getting up and down from his horse and knocked by the horn on the saddle—all happening during his time as ferrier for the 10th Calvary.

When asked by pension board examiners to provide verification of birth, Hollins explained, "My mother was a colored woman in Tennessee—a slave—and affiant's father Jack Hollins bought affiant's mother. Father died in Tennessee, so he was told by his mother that he was born on the first day of March 1844."

Columbus applied to the State Soldiers Home in Orting, Washington, on January 19, 1905, when old age and disability limited his capacity for manual labor. Approval to enter the home was given on February 5. He stayed there until his death in 1919.

Of the things he left behind, an old cheap pocket watch was given to his friend Mrs. Verna L. Morgan.

He never married and left no known descendants.

NICHOLAS JOHNSON

January 18, 1848–July 4, 1934
New Castle, Henry County, Kentucky—Orting, Pierce County, Washington
Orting Soldiers Home Cemetery
Orting, Pierce County, Washington
Private, Company I, 124th Regiment, United States Colored Infantry
February 23, 1865–December 4, 1865
Lexington, Kentucky—Louisville, Kentucky
Corporal, Troup B, 24th United States Army
(formerly 40th First United States Army Infantry)
January 8, 1867–October 31, 1869
Henry County, Kentucky—Fort Bliss, El Paso, Texas

Joseph Foree of Kenton County, Kentucky, owned Emeline and her son, Nicholas. At the age of sixteen, Nicholas left his home to become a member of the U.S. Colored Troops. He spent his military years as a cook and steward. During his time in the service, his regiment stayed at Camp

Nelson doing garrison duty and never saw any battle action. Nicholas did not muster out at the same time as his comrades. He entered the camp's hospital in July and remained there until he was well enough to leave in November. In his deposition dated November 23, 1908, he said:

> *The first peculiar sensation of pain I found in my teeth, was, while I was in the Hospital at Camp Nelson near Nicholasville, Kentucky, in September 1865. I left the Hospital in November 1865, and went to my home in Georgetown, Kentucky to recuperate my health as it was in a very poor condition.*[226]

His toothaches amounted to eventual decay and removal of his teeth. To deaden the pain, he treated the teeth with creosote. In one of his physical examinations in 1908, the physicians noted that he only had three teeth left in his mouth. After two years of getting healthy, Nicholas enlisted in the army, 41st Infantry.

On July 28, 1866, the federal government passed the Army Reorganization Act, which provided a framework for the army following the massive change the institution underwent during the Civil War. The act also specifically called for the formation of six all-Black regiments to be permanently established within the army: two cavalry units (9th and 10th) and four infantry units (38th, 49th, 4th and 41st). In March 1869, Congress again ordered a reorganization of the army, mandating among other things that these four infantry units should be amalgamated into just two regiments. The 24th was created by combining the 38th and the 41st.[227]

Assigned as a cook for Troop B of the 24th, Nicholas reported to Brownsville, Texas, for the eventual trip to White Ranch at Brazos Santiago via the transport *Agnes* and steamer *St. Mary*. The troop guarded the mouth of the Rio Grande from Indians and bandit movements between Texas and Mexico.

During this time, the soldiers continued to perform garrison duties—including daily fatigue, construction, guard duty and so on—along with duties outside the post such as securing the mail and stage routes, road repair, hanging telegraph wire and almost whatever else was required. During one of these missions, a small band of Indians on horseback approached a detachment of soldiers and attacked them. The soldiers responded well and repelled the attack.[228]

By September 1869 and in time for his discharge, Troop B was ordered to Fort Bliss, Texas, near El Paso and consolidated with Troop A of the 38th

Infantry to form the 24th Infantry. After discharge at the end of October, he moved to Fort Clarke to run a restaurant. He worked as a servant for Lieutenant Albin of the 24th Colored Infantry and Captain Loud of the 9th Cavalry, and he worked at the Alexander Post Trader. He stayed in Texas for nearly twenty years before moving to Santa Fe, New Mexico.

In Santa Fe, he worked for Mr. P. Ramsey, proprietor of the Palace Hotel, for six years as the hotel's primary cook. He met and married Esther Depp in 1887 before moving to Los Angeles, California, to work at the Argyle Hotel as a cook and his wife as the hotel's maid.

On September 29, 1889, Nicholas and Esther entered the state of Washington and made the city of Tacoma their permanent residence. They found work at the Chilberg Restaurant. For the next ten years, the effects of the Civil War began affecting his everyday life. His wife's health was also in decline.

On February 29, 1908, he applied for his Civil War pension for health issues. Examination by three physicians in July 1908 concluded that "he could not do manual labor for the following reasons: senility, diabetes, rheumatism, lumbago, sciatica, heart, piles, and 'not due to vicious habits.'" While he waited for approval of the pension board, he notified it that he temporarily relocated to the city of Wapato in North Yakima County, Washington, working in the local hotel as a chef.

For the next eight years, Nicholas experienced additional health issues. He was stricken with paralytic strokes from which he partially recovered. The strokes reduced the use of his left side and forced him to use a cane to walk. He applied for admission to Orting's Soldiers Home, and approval was granted on August 16, 1913. For the next five years, he was plagued with more strokes that weakened him even more, and to add to his burden, his wife, Esther, required additional caretaking. He utilized his neighbors for a while and was granted two furloughs from the Soldiers Home to help with his wife's care. Esther died in October 1928.

Nicholas became a permanent resident of the home and did not leave unless assisted. He met his next wife, Alice Brooks, at the home when she was visiting another inmate. Three years later, they were married. She kept her residence at his home on South Trafton Street in Tacoma, Washington.

Nicholas died in 1934; Alice died in 1936.

SAMUEL F. JOHNSON

October 29, 1846–May 7, 1912
Cape May, Cape May County, New Jersey—Seattle, Washington
Cremated—Place of Interment Unknown
Private, Company H, 127ᵗʰ Regiment, United States Colored Infantry
Private, Company A, 127ᵗʰ Regiment, United States Colored Infantry
Norristown, Pennsylvania—Brazos Santiago, Texas
September 3, 1864–October 20, 1865
United States Navy
USS Potomac *and USS St.* Louis, *1867–1869*

Samuel Johnson enlisted in the Union army as a substitute for Tilghman Diebert of North Whitehall, Pennsylvania. The members of this regiment may have seen the surrender of Robert E. Lee and his army.

After Johnson's military service was completed, he enlisted in the navy in 1867 for a term of two years. During those years, he was assigned to the USS *Potomac* and USS *St. Louis*. Upon completion of his service, he spent the next seventeen years on the sea. In the latter part of those seventeen years, Samuel became part of the crew of the steamer *Bowhead*. The *Bowhead*, a whaling ship, was originally built in San Francisco and moored there. In 1891, a second *Bowhead* was built.

In a General Affidavit, Samuel stated, "[I] lost [my] Navy discharges in a wreck in 1884, on the steamer *Bowhead*. Also [my] trunk and everything [I] had was lost in the wreck in the Arctic Ocean." A wreck report dated October 14, 1884, for the American steamship *Bowhead* indicated

Steamer *Bowhead*, whaling ship. It sunk in the northern Arctic Ocean in 1883. *Courtesy of Wikimedia Commons.*

that at 3 PM on August 10, 1884, while cruising in the Arctic Ocean and having sailed from "Omalaska" with shipmaster Everett E. Smith, a crew of 49 and cargo of oil and ivory, weighing 35 tons valued at $10,000, suffered a total loss. The vessel was valued at $150,000 and was owned by Pacific Steam whaling Arctic Oil Company. The locality of the casualty was given as "Lat 70-33N, Long 161-27W" (new Point Barrow) and the nature of the casualty was described as "crushed in the ice."[229]

The *San Francisco Examiner* reported:

> *The weather was calm and foggy on the morning of the day that the casualty occurred. The engineer reported that the boiler tubes were leaking and the occasion was considered a favorable one to blow off steam and make repairs....The ice was then noticed to be coming down, and an engineer endeavor was made to haul her away. The attempt failed, and she was caught surrounded in the ice and crushed.*[230]...*The entire crew was rescued by the steamship Balena.*

"Shipping Articles and Crew Lists, 1854–1950," located in the National Archives Records and Administration in San Bruno, California, had the crew list for the bark *Bowhead* that sailed from the Port of San Francisco on December 15, 1883. It listed "Samuel JOHNSON born ca. 1851 in Philadelphia, employed as the cook of the vessel."[231]

It is hard to say what happened to Samuel between 1886 and 1894 before he showed up in Seattle. He was living at the foot of Virginia Street, close to the piers on Puget Sound. For the next six years, he obtained jobs as a

Repairing nets. *Courtesy of Port of Seattle, Fisherman Terminal History.*

fisherman until health issues affected his ability to fish; he found a job as a janitor working at the Haller Building on 2nd Avenue. Johnson was working with another Civil War soldier, Joseph P. Bennett, and they eventually became good friends.

Like many other Civil War soldiers, Johnson started his pension application process and was subjected to examinations by three physicians. These physicians found that he was afflicted with rheumatism, and "we find no other disability to exist." Initially rejected for lack of apparent disability, he reapplied in May 1910 and was approved at a rate of twelve dollars.

Samuel worked at the Haller Building as a janitor until his death. When he died intestate, his friend Joseph Bennett hired an attorney and petitioned the court to become executor of Samuel's estate. His estate consisted of an insurance policy of $178.75. After all expenditures were noted ($183.75), Joseph Bennett paid from his personal funds the balance due of $5.[232]

Samuel Johnson left no living descendants. His first marriage, to Martha Ann Merrils on July 30, 1861, in Huntington, Pennsylvania, produced no children; she died in New Jersey in 1864.

SAMUEL LARKINS

1844–March 13, 1910
Trigg County, Kentucky—Orting, Pierce County, Washington
Soldiers Home Cemetery
Orting, Pierce County, Washington
Private, Company K, 101st Regiment, United States Colored Infantry
January 16, 1865–January 21, 1866
Clarksville, Tennessee

Samuel was born into slavery in Kentucky. He reported on his life as a slave in a statement within his pension file dated July 10, 1901:

I was a slave as I was informed when I found myself with Lucretia Holloday [sic] (an old maid) and then after she died her brother Irwin Holloday [sic] took me for a while as property and shortly after, I run away and enlisted in the army.[233]

Lucretia Hollowell was the sister-in-law who owned Samuel. Lucretia on the 1850 slave census had a six-year-old male who was most likely Samuel.

She died in March 1851, and Samuel was given/sold to her brother Dr. Irwin S. Hollowell of Caldwell County, Kentucky, just north of Trigg County. There was a sixteen-year-old mulatto male on the 1860 slave schedule for Irwin Hollowell. This sixteen-year-old was most likely Samuel.

A will for Lucretia Hollowell decided the disposition of Samuel Larkins:

> *3rd. I will and desire that my executor sell my negro boy Sam either publickly or privately as he may think best and shortly after my decease sell my perishible estate and apply fifty dollars....The perishible property towards...up the family...yard and take a sufficient sum from said perishable estate and from the proceeds of the sale of my Negro boy Sam to defray my funeral expenses and to put grave stones to my grave, the residue of the proceeds of the sale of my Negro Sam and perishible estate I give to my brothers and sisters to be equally divided amongst them after paying my brother Noah Hollowell the sum of about twenty dollars which I owe him and other debts and expenses.*[234]

Sam was not the only one in his family to escape slavery and join the colored infantry. Brothers James, Thomas and John all joined the same regiment as Sam, Company K, 101st U.S. Colored Infantry, on the same date, January 8, 1865, and mustered out on January 21, 1866. After mustering out, the brothers became farmers in Kentucky. James and Samuel both married and had children. James and Sam went their separate ways. James went through many enlistments into the Regular Army, and thirty-four years later, he became a resident in Phoenix, Arizona. The whereabouts of the other brothers after 1870 have been difficult to discover. In a pension deposition dated March 1, 1904, Samuel gave more details of his life as a slave and noted a brother:

> *My name is Samuel Larkins. I was born a Slave in Trigg Co Kentucky but was sold to William Larkins when a child & took his name. Was raised in Christian Co. Ky during the time I was in slavery. I was sold twice. My Mother was sold when I was a child & I have never been able to find any trace of her. My brother was sold to a Planter by the name of Robert Hopkins of Christian Co. Ky. I took him with me & both joined same Co K 101st—he died while in the service in Wilson Hospital in Nashville Tenn.*[235]

As a child, he and his brothers were subjected to "King's Evil," or scrofula. A colored woman said that he had it because of the "sins of his parents" and would have it all his life.

In Samuel's initial examination, he told the physician:

Soon after the close of the war [I] *commenced to have rheumatism in the left knees. Had it in other part of body Sometimes free from it for a long time. Once for seven years, knee swells and become painful, leg also swells Had chancres, boppers, gonorrhea....We* [physicians] *find that than aggregate permanent disability for earning a support by manual, not all labor is due to rheumatism, and senility not due to vicious habits and calls for a rating of $6.00.*[236]

Every year for the next six years, Samuel was required to be examined. He complained about the same ailments. The physician gave him the same results of the examination. He could not get more than six dollars.

According to a physician's affidavit dated February 27, 1906, the doctor at Soldiers Home in Orting, Washington, described his examination of Sam:

[I]*njured in ankles left one is worse than right in such a degree that he walks with considerable difficulty. He claims he received this injury while in the service at Henderson, Tenn May 28, 1865 being caught in the frog of a railroad while trying to save themselves from an attack of the enemy. In addition, he sustained a gunshot wound on his left arm in early August 1865 at Henderson, T.N. His examining physician noted a scar on the left arm where a gunshot "ball" had been removed.*[237]

He returned to Kentucky after the war ended. He met and married Katherine "Kittie" Hawkins in Hopkinsville in 1867. They were the parents of three children—two sons and one daughter. Kittie died in 1883. With his children grown, he left Kentucky and made his way to Washington State via Arkansas (Little Rock, Pine Bluff, Fort Smith, Hot Springs and Athens), arriving in Washington in about 1889 or 1890.

For six years, Samuel was the owner of a barbershop in the New England Hotel in Orting, Washington. He applied for admission to Orting Soldiers Home in June 1902 when he realized that the deterioration of his health caused his inability to do manual labor. Approved by the commander, he became a resident. For a short time, the commander evicted Larkins from the home for unruly behavior. After a letter of apology and another application in 1907, approval for re-admission to the home was granted, and he stayed until his death:

Then is due you, as well as the Supt of the State Soldiers Home a full expression of my regrets at conducts that I now see was irregular and wrong and would not occur except for that usual deficit in the old soldier's intemperance....I shall in the future obey every rule and regulation laid down for my guidance while in the home.[238]

It seems that Samuel was not the only one that disturbed the peace of the home:

[T]*here were disturbing outside influences. There were five licensed saloons and drinking places in Orting which were easily approachable by the "Boardwalk." Apparently, these places were being frequented by the Home residents, with the proprietors not discouraging them. Consequently, the men very often returned back to the Home intoxicated and proceeded to disrupt the discipline already so difficult to sustain under the Home's overcrowded condition.*[239]

Several years after Samuel's death, a claim for his pension was made by a man named Frank Larkins on behalf of Sallie Larkins of Kentucky. Frank on several occasions claimed to be a "friend" and at other times a "son" of Sallie. She was resident of an insane asylum in Kentucky. With her mental state in mind, the details of her life through her own words made the process of application difficult.

In various instances, she claimed that she married to Samuel in 1849 and later changed it to 1866; that he lived with her until his death; that he deserted her and their children; and, finally, that he was a member of the 16th U.S. Colored Infantry. Samuel was born in 1844 and far too young to be married in 1849. Marriage in 1866 could not be proven since there had been two fires in 1866 at the Trigg County Courthouse. He died in Washington State, not Kentucky. He was already in Washington prior to 1890. In addition, his children were with Katherine Hawkins Larkins. He was a member of the 101st U.S. Colored Infantry.

Frank Larkins attempted to find individuals to confirm Sallie's statements regarding her marriage and relationship with Samuel. Xenphone Radcliffe testified on November 3, 1912, "Sam deserted Sallie about 1894." Bill Howard testified on March 3, 1914, "They lived together until his death." Frank Larkins denied knowing the other children of Samuel Larkins.

The pension board rejected Sallie's application on June 2, 1913, for failure "to show service of claimant's husband as alleged." However, Frank tried again to secure a pension payout for Sallie. A letter in Samuel's pension file documented the many attempts to confirm Sallie's assertions.

There seemed to have been a conscious effort to perpetrate a conspiracy to get money from the government. After all this effort, Sallie died on September 10, 1915, in the Western State Hospital in Hopkinsville, Kentucky, of "exhaustion from psychosis of period of involution and senility." She was buried at the hospital's cemetery. Frank Larkins's last correspondence with any governmental official was in 1914.

Within Larkins's patient file at the home was a receipt from George Tibbetts to Ella M. Brown for the sum of $235.65. This was part of Samuel's estate that executrix Ella received as part of her administration of his estate. She posted notification often over five weeks in the local newspaper requesting persons who had some interest in Samuel's estate assets. A court date of February 3, 1912, was set for the distribution of those assets. Since Ella was the only heir in Samuel's will, dated August 14, 1909, she received all his assets, including a barber's chair, a small mirror and cash. The total estate was valued at $275.65. Ella M. Brown was a resident at the Soldier's Home's Colony.[240] She was admitted as a widow of Civil War soldier Ansel H. Brown, a private in Company D, 10th Regiment, Michigan cavalry.[241]

Samuel Larkins left no descendants in Washington but may have some in Kentucky.

CHARLES A. MORGAN

1848–May 1, 1903
Athens, Athens County, Ohio—Pierce County, Washington
Soldiers Home Cemetery
Orting, Pierce County, Washington
Private, Company F, 17th Regiment, United States Colored Infantry
August 15, 1864–September 29, 1865
Prescott, Wisconsin—Nashville, Tennessee

This is the third soldier in this group who had fewer than fifty pages in his pension file. The file had little to no information from which to write a thorough history of his prewar or postwar life.

Charles was born to parents Moses and Nancy Morgan, who were free persons of color in Athens, Ohio. He was one of eight identified children born between the years 1838 and 1867.

He entered the service at age sixteen and was described as five feet, nine inches with a dark complexion and black eyes and hair. Charles does not mention his time in the war, nor does he acknowledge any wartime injuries that occurred.

His regiment was engaged in a skirmish on December 15 and 16, 1864, just south of Nashville against General John B. Hood's army:

> The 17th USCT [was] to take up the momentum of the advance by sweeping past the enemy's exposed spur. Colonel Shafter's men dutifully moved forward, coming abreast of the silent enemy lunette to the right. Only when these troops got to the railroad line and found their way blocked by a deep ravine did the Rebel cannoneers in the lunette open fire. At the same moment, Confederate infantry and artillery swung out from the entrenched line directly in front of Shafter's men, catching the 17th USCT in a devastating fire from front, right flank, and rear. "It was an awful battle," Shafter wrote to his sister afterward. "We had the negroes in our trap," related a Georgia soldier on the hill, "and when we commenced firing on them, complete demoralization followed. Many jumped into the [railroad] cut and were either killed or captured." In his report, Shafter stated that the 17th USCT had been "soon obliged to fall back, which was done in rather a disorderly manner."[242]

The regimental return reported two commissioned officers killed and four wounded; thirteen enlisted men killed; one missing, supposed killed; and fifty-eight wounded.

At his discharge, Charles was given the balance of his bounty in the amount of $33.34 and "Retain[ed] Gun & Accoutrements under the provisions of Special Orders 101 War Dept current series Entitled to Transportation & Subsistence to place of original enrollment."

He returned to Ohio and married Sarah E. Leonard, who brought to the marriage a son, William Stuttle. Charles acknowledged William as his own in a document at his admission to Orting Soldiers Home Hospital. Morgan's whereabouts from 1880 to 1890 are unknown.

He applied for a pension on November 29, 1890, while still living in Minnesota. The application process for the pension did not go well for Charles. He initially filled out his "Declaration for Invalid Pension" on November 20, 1890. He claimed that he was "wholly unable to earn a support by reason of and is now suffering from rheumatism, disease of the throat, kidneys, eyes, back and catarrh."

Multiple attempts to have Charles examined by physicians went unanswered. He finally had his examination on July 1, 1891, in Minnesota. The physicians confirmed that he was suffering from the multiple medical complaints. Sometime after his initial physical examination, he moved to Superior, Wisconsin. Letters sent to him went unclaimed. Ultimately, he was located, and he reapplied for his pension on August 5, 1897. Again, the pension board had difficulty reaching him for a physical examination. The pension board rejected his application soon thereafter, and a certificate number was not issued, thus denying him the much-needed pension money.

A statement in his Orting patient file suggested that Charles was in Seattle in 1898 alone. He said that his wife died prior to moving to Seattle and that his son, William, was now living in Minneapolis, Minnesota. Charles, for a while, worked as a barber for C.A. Johnson in Orting, Washington.

At some point toward the end of 1902, he started to experience some medical issues. A doctor admitted him to Providence Hospital on Madison Street in Seattle, and he was attended by Dr. R.M. Davis, a surgeon. Dr. Davis communicated with Orting Soldiers Home and requested Charles's admission, as staying at the hospital was becoming untenable. Charles applied on December 9, 1902, and was admitted on February 14, 1903. He was dead by May.

Charles Morgan has no living descendants in Washington but may have some by his stepson, William, in Minnesota.

DAVID STARKHILL SLAUGHTER

March 25, 1845–March 5, 1910
Danville, Boyle County, Kentucky—Tacoma, Pierce County, Washington
Oakwood Hill Cemetery
Tacoma, Pierce County, Washington
Sgt. Company F, 114th Regiment, United States Colored Infantry
May 30, 1864–April 2, 1867
Camp Nelson, Jessamine County, Kentucky—Brazos de Santiago, Texas

David Slaughter was born into slavery to James and Susan Stillwell/Russell Slaughter, under the ownership of John Stodgill of Boyle County, Kentucky. On August 2, 1892, he said:

I enlisted under the name of David Starkhill. It was intended for "Stodghill," but the clerk got it Starkhill and I had to answer to that name. After I came out of the service, I took my own name, David S. Slaughter.[243]

When he enlisted in 1864, he was sent to Camp Nelson in Kentucky, a training camp for incoming African American soldiers. He spent the next three years moving around. In February 1865, he and his company/ regiment marched their way to Richmond as part of the siege of that city. Within the next few days, they marched to Appomattox to become part of the seizure of that city and most probably saw the surrender of Robert E. Lee to U.S. Grant on April 9, 1865.[244]

On May 3, the company marched from Petersburg, Virginia, to City Point, Virginia. On May 31, it embarked on the transport *CC Seary* at City Point, and on June 24, it disembarked at Brazos, Santiago, Texas, and marched that night to Whites Ranch on the Rio Grande, about twelve miles. On June 28, the men marched ten miles to Brownsville, Texas. They encamped for the night and the next morning resumed the march, arriving within three miles of Brownsville, Texas. They took muster at Brownsville.

For the next six months, the company and regiment remained encamped outside Brownsville, Texas. At the beginning of 1866, the company did guard and fatigue duty at Arsenal Ranch and Redmond Ranch until finally being stationed themselves at Ringgold Barracks in July 1866. Fort Ringgold, the southernmost installation of the western tier of forts constructed at the end of the Mexican-American War, stood guard for nearly a century over the Rio Grande and Rio Grande City.[245]

David married Nannie Davis in Boyle County, Kentucky, on December 21, 1869. Between the years 1871 and 1892, they had eight children: Ophelia, David, John, James, Detroit, Ralph, Alice and Charles.

Slaughter would have seen the many soldiers suffering from scurvy entering the hospital for treatment while working as hospital steward at Ringgold Barracks, Texas. The army, for whatever reason, denied the seriousness of the disease. Few agreed that the disease existed:

Stacy Hemingway, surgeon to the 41st US Colored Infantry, in an article published in the Chicago Medical Examiner, did suggest that the illness [scurvy] was not associated with the innate characteristics of Black people. Hemingway had seen within his own regiment the beginning of the disease in his men as they boarded crowded water transports, and it was getting progressively worse as those transports arrived some weeks later in

Texas. The rations of those men typically consisted of salt pork, hardtack and water with little or no fresh fruits or vegetables.[246]

David Slaughter also suffered from scurvy and rheumatism. A doctor reported that at "Ringgold Barracks, TX in fall of 1865 incurred rheumatism and resulting disease of heart, scurvy and diarrhea, malaria and resulting indigestion, dystrophia…also incurred in the disease of the throat and nose."[247]

When he was discharged, he returned to Danville, Kentucky, and engaged to learn the trade of plasterer. "I studied for a preacher while I worked at plastering. When I completed my studies, I discontinued the business of plasterer and devoted myself to my profession a preacher of the Gospel and have so continued ever since I have been wholly unfit for heavy manual labor in each year since discharge."[248] While living in Muncie, Indiana, David hired attorney H.T. Kincaid for a fee of twenty-five dollars to represent him in his application for an increase in his pension. An application was sent to Veterans Affairs on January 13, 1893:

[A]*lleges that at Ringgold Barracks, Texas in fall of 1865, he incurred rheumatism and resulting disease of heart, scurvy, and diarrhea, malaria, and resulting in indigestion and dyspepsia. He also incurred in the service disease of throat and nose.*[249]

He applied nineteen times within a span of seventeen years to get an increase of his pension monies, with multiple rejections because he could not provide proof of the source of his Civil War disabilities. One of his applications for increase was rejected on April 27, 1901: "No satisfactory evidence of incurrence in service of the alleged…and claimant declares his inability to furnished competent proof to establish his claim."[250] He still maintained the small pension of six to ten dollars per month. At his death in 1909, he was receiving twelve dollars per month.

As a widow of a Civil War soldier, his wife, Nannie Davis Slaughter, was entitled to apply for his pension. She was living in Washington State when she applied on September 21, 1910. Nannie's application was almost at once approved. Her payment of thirty dollars began in October 1910 and continued until her death in Tacoma, Washington, in the month of December 1927.

David's son David T. applied for a minor's entitlement against his father's pension on the assumption that his mother had received the widow's certificate. In a letter dated December 11, 1928, to the pension board,

David T. requested his father's pension. By that time, David T. was fifty-four years old, blind and crippled. "I have been informed that I, a disabled son is intitled to some consideration from your honorable department hoping to hear some information from you soon as I am gratefully in need of help now."[251] The pension board's reply to the letter on February 19, 1929, was terse: "I have to advise you that you have no possible title to pension under any existing law providing for a minor child of a soldier, for the reason that you are over sixteen."[252]

David left descendants in Kentucky.

SNOHOMISH COUNTY

JOHN CLARK (ALIAS CICERO HUNTER)

May 10, 1841–1916
Owensboro, Daviess County, Kentucky—Everett, Snohomish County, Washington
Evergreen Cemetery
Everett, Snohomish County, Washington
Private, Company K, 32nd Regiment, United States Colored Infantry
October 20, 1864–April 6, 1866
Springfield, Tennessee—Springfield, Tennessee

Cicero Hunter, also known as John Clark, the son of Charles and Kitty Hall Hunter, was born on May 10, 1841, in Owensboro, Kentucky. He was born into a family of nine children—most died. The only children left were Cicero, Jessee and Atha.

The abolitionist Cassius M. Clay, son of General Green Clay and distant cousin of Henry Clay, owned Kitty's mother, Lucy Clay. In about 1844, Cassius freed a number of slaves, one of whom was Lucy. She in turn purchased her grandson Cicero when he was about five years old from Thomas Hall Pointer of Kentucky. Cicero and his grandmother lived together under the guardianship of George Clark for several years. Just before James Buchanan was elected president (1856), Lucy passed away, leaving fifteen-year-old Cicero to be bound out to George Clark and later to Robert G. Moorman until the age of twenty-one.

During the next few years, Kitty and Charles and his brother lived with separate owners. Kitty lived with Frank Lockett Hall until 1858, when she escaped and ran to Canada. Charles lived with Dr. Frances Fitzhugh Conway, the local physician, until 1860, when he found out that Kitty had gone to Canada. He pursued her and eventually found her. Nicholas Bosley and his family owned brothers Jessee and Atha.

When the war came, Charles and Kitty entered the United States via Detroit, Michigan, in 1863. The parents found their three sons and were reunited in Kalamazoo, Michigan. By 1864, the men of the Hunter family had joined the Union army: John/Cicero joined Company K, 32nd U.S. Colored Infantry; Atha became a private in Company C, 8th U.S. Colored Infantry; and Jessee along with their father, Charles, enlisted into Company E, 28th U.S. Colored Infantry—Jessee as a private and Charles as a sergeant. Of this group of men, Jessee was the only one who did not survive the war.

While in the care of George Clark, Cicero was known as Cicero Clark until he was given the nickname of John. He used the name John Clark during the Civil War, but he returned to Cicero Hunter at the reuniting of his parents and siblings. This name change proved in later years to cause him much difficulty in his application for a pension.

In Cicero's pension file of 494 pages, a General Affidavit dated November 30, 1900, tells of his injury during a military incident:

> *While in the service of the US on Bulls Island S.C. in the year 1865 (about Feb or March) on a charge, I was barefooted (and nearly naked) and I hit my foot on a snag or injured the foot in some manner. I felt the pain but I could not stop and had to keep going. There was no Surgeon with us and a hospital steward who treated me is now dead, and I paid the last money I had to an old woman to look after the wound and she must be dead.*[253]

Right after his service in the war, he hired on as a second cook on the *Stars & Stripes* merchant vessel—destination Cuba. On two occasions, he made two trips to Liverpool, England, on the *Saxon* and the *Pennsylvania* as a mess room steward. When he returned to Pennsylvania, he worked on Montclair Street in a Philadelphia saloon owned by John Hamilton. This employment lasted six months before he tried to run his own saloon on 6th and Lombard Streets with the help of Josh Eddie; the business only lasted three months. Several of his other jobs included working as a steward at the local police station and working for Dilkes & Pearson, a produce market, for four or five years. For a few summers, Cicero worked for a Mr.

Broadhead at the Delaware Water and Gas Company. He left Philadelphia in 1873 and continued his journey west to Indianapolis. From 1883 to 1885, Cicero was a resident of Indianapolis, Indiana, working as a laborer and porter.[254]

On March 4, 1889, the inauguration of President Benjamin Harrison was an event of some note. *The Appeal*, dated March 16, 1889, noted local citizens who were present for that event: "Messrs. Cicero Hunter, W.R. Rogers, J. Hill and H. Freeman returned Monday last from Washington D.C., where they attended the inauguration."

Cicero's first marriage was to the former Mary Knox, who brought her daughter, Bessie, into the marriage. Their marriage was celebrated on April 30, 1888, in Indianapolis, Indiana. His marriage to Mary ended in her divorcing Cicero in 1892. Mary died a few years later. Bessie's marriage was announced in *The Appeal*:

> *Mr. and Mrs. Cicero Hunter wish to announce the marriage of Mr. Eugene R. Jeffrey and their daughter Miss Bessie Hunter. The wedding will take place in April.*[255] *Mr. Jean* [sic] *Jeffries and Miss Bessie Hunter were united in marriage on last Tuesday evening at 1312 Third avenue south, at 9:00 o'clock. Rev. T. Reeves officiated.*[256]

Cicero married for a second time to the former Annie Thompson in Whatcom County, Washington, on August 20, 1890. Two children were born into the marriage: Emma and Henry.

It is not often that photographs are found in pension files, but his file actually includes one. According to Cicero, he was photographed twice in his life: one, a daguerreotype, was taken before the war. The other, shown here, was taken several years after the Civil War by his landlady at the time. Even in a deposition by his brother Atha Hunter, dated August 11, 1902, the photos were talked about:

Photo of Clark, reportedly taken by his landlady, circa 1885. *Author's collection.*

> *I have two pictures of my brother one in tintype that was taken before the war and the other a photograph which was taken about twenty years after his discharge. Here they are. (Defendant thereupon produced the two pictures as above described) You can take them for the purpose of identification but I*

would like to have them returned to me at this place when the Pension Office has properly found my brother.[257]

Cicero's photo was used by the examiner to try to name him as John Clark. When Captain Newton Plummer examined two of the photos of John Clark, he remarked:

I have examined two photographs shown me but cannot recognize them as the pictures of any one I ever knew. Yet the face of the smaller picture looks a little familiar. Having been informed that it is a likeness of John Clark who was in my co. I am still unable to recognize it. I have no distinct recollection of Clark as a member of the Co.[258]

Everything was working against him, including examinations by physicians to figure out if his health issues would allow him to get a pension. The physicians found "no ratable" diseases that would prevent him from doing manual labor.

For many years (1895–1903), Cicero battled with the pension bureau and special examiners to get a pension for his part in the Civil War. He gave the examiners names of individual soldiers, members of his own family and neighbors in Minnesota where he lived most of his life. These individuals only added to the confusion about his two names—John Clark and Cicero Hunter. By 1903, he had exhausted every effort to have his pension approved. A letter from the Law Division gave the reasons for rejection: "This claim was rejected, after a thorough special investigation, in September, 1903, on the ground that the claimant had failed, after a thorough special examination, to prove his identity with the person who rendered the service under the name of John Clark."[259]

Not being happy about the decision, Cicero started a letter writing campaign to government employees of the pension bureau to get the rejection reversed. On June 30, 1903, he wrote, "I enlisted under the name of John Clark so my mother would not take me out of the army." Within a few months, he received a response from the bureau that affirmed the rejection under the Act of June 27, 1890, and the Act of February 6, 1907, for failure to prove that he was John Clark. He tried again in 1911 and received same response: "Your claim is rejected."

That confusion also contributed to not having a proper headstone at the time of his burial. With the help of a community activist, a Civil War headstone was acquired in 2011. Cicero maintained his residence in Everett and may have descendants in Minnesota.

ALFORD (ALFRED) SAMUELS

1818–October 10, 1903
Bullitt, Nelson County, Kentucky—Everett, Snohomish County, Washington
Greenwood Cemetery
Everett, Snohomish County, Washington
August 27, 1864–June 15, 1865
Company H, 107th United States Colored Infantry
Memphis, Shelby County, Tennessee—Goldsboro, Wayne County, North Carolina

Alfred was born to George and Harriet Samuels. He was the eldest of five children, along with three others whose names are known: Lucinda, Isaac and George. They lived for the most part in Nelson County, Kentucky. At the time of his enlistment in the Union army, Mary Samuels, the daughter of Sexton R. Samuels, owned him. On Sexton's probate inventory dated September 16, 1861, Alfred, age thirty-two, was listed with his children (Tyler, William, Lucy, Charity and Charley) by his first mate, Sarah.[260] Mary Samuels inherited six slaves.[261] These slaves were previously given to Sexton's wife, Mary Barager, as a gift from her father. Alfred was mated with Jane (Wise). It is not known if three children on the inventory were Jane's before she cohabitated with Alfred or if they were the couple's own children. She did assume the parenting of Alfred's first children.

Alfred was thirty years old when he enlisted in the U.S. Colored Infantry for a period of three years. He was described as having dark eyes, hair and complexion and was five feet, three and a half inches tall. His regiment was stationed in Louisville, Kentucky, until October before transferring to City Point, Virginia, via Baltimore, Maryland. In late 1864, the 107th USCI occupied a position on the line around Petersburg, with 40 percent of the men armed with imitation Enfield rifled muskets, made

Slave inventory for Sexton Robert Samuels, dated 1861. *Courtesy of Familysearch.org.*

in Philadelphia, which had a defective mainspring and often would not fire.[262] This regiment engaged the enemy at Fort Fisher, North Carolina. At the time, the 107th belonged to the 24th Army Corps, 3rd Division, under the command of Brigadier General Charles J. Paine. They assaulted Fort Fisher and were victorious along with other divisions. While this battle was raging on, Alfred Samuels was spending his time in the field hospital recuperating from rheumatism and jaundice; there was no notation that he ever engaged the enemy.

After the war, Alfred's former slave owner, Mary Samuels, applied for compensation for the loss of her slave. The application for compensation signed by Mary on March 21, 1867, was used by this writer as proof of her ownership when she offered Samuel for enlistment. Such manumission documents are unique to the records of the USCT. To help recruiting in the states of Maryland, Missouri, Tennessee and Kentucky, the War Department issued General Order No. 329 on October 3, 1863. Section 6 of the order stated:

> [I]f any citizen should offer his or her slave for enlistment into the military service, that person would, "if such slave be accepted, receive from the recruiting officer a certificate thereof, and become entitled to compensation for the service or labor of said slave, not exceeding the sum of three hundred dollars, upon filing a valid deed of manumission and of release, and making satisfactory proof of title." For this reason, records of manumission are contained in the compiled service records....Required evidence included title to the slave and loyalty to the Union government. Further, every owner signed an oath of allegiance to the government of the United States. Each statement was witnessed and certified.[263]

If she collected her compensation, a record of that transaction was not found.

After the war, Alfred returned to Kentucky briefly. He "took up" with Jane Wise again. There were six additional children born before this family moved to McLean County, Illinois. The last three of their children were born in Illinois. Sadly, Jane died in about 1859. He married his third wife, Rebecca Grissom, on September 7, 1893. She died later that year on December 22. With three adult children living in Washington, he had moved to Everett by late 1902 and lived with children John, Mary and Rosabelle.

Alfred Samuels's pension file contained information about his health issues that he experienced from the last days of his service in the army and the first days after he went home. The pension file contains mainly depositions of friends, comrades and family members explaining what his health was before entering the army and his health issues after his military service.

Age and the effects of the war caused him much distress. He remarked that during the months of September and October 1864 near Richmond, Virginia, he spent most of that time exposed to the elements, including "sleeping on the damp ground and in the cold—which [he] was necessarily required to do in the discharge of his duties as a soldier."[264] He would spend many months in the field hospital at Point of Rocks, Virginia.

His brothers Isaac and George Samuels, in a joint sworn statement on October 31, 1888, before the clerk of the court in McLean County, Illinois, testified to their brother's "physical condition prior to and at the time of his enrollment and enlistment in the military service and they know that he was then in good sound physical health and was free from rheumatism, yellow jaundice and those eyes and that his hearing in both ears was then good."

In multiple physical examinations, Alfred complained of getting these diseases because of his exposure to bad weather and food that was inedible. These diseases followed him when he mustered out of the service and returned to his hometown in Illinois.

With this exposure, he claimed that rheumatism had affected his quality of life since the war. He said he was not able to do manual labor to provide for his family. After he was seen by Dr. W.C. Cox, his personal physician, in a letter dated April 24, 1903, the doctor told of an emergency visit on November 2, 1902, during which he found

> *Samuels suffering from paralysis of the entire right side including the tongue. In the opinion the affiant the paralysis was due to an apoplectic stroke the result of old age [85]. The paralysis was so severe as to confine the patient to his bed for a number of weeks.... [A]t present...is gradually getting over the paralysis but...he will not, owing to his advanced age ever entirely recover.*[265]

The following year, Alfred was examined by his physician on an emergency basis again. Dr. Cox found other ailments affecting Alfred:

> *His general condition is poor due, perhaps, in the main to his having lost all his teeth in the upper jaw thereby making mastication very difficult producing also poor digestion. He also noted that he was doing better after a*

Frederick Samuels, eighth child of Alfred Samuels (1868–1930). *Photo in possession of L. Kimbourgh.*

paralyzing stroke affecting his right side. Alfred still could not lift his right arm but could walk a short distance.[266]

He died later in 1903 from apoplexy.

Contact was made through Ancestry.com with his great-great-granddaughter L.K. Kimbrough. She was able to complete some of Alfred's family history, and it was discovered that she was also related to another Civil War soldier featured in this writing, Jessee Donaldson.

Alfred was a member of William T. Sherman Post 146, Grand Army of the Republic (GAR), in Bloomington, Illinois.

Alfred left behind many descendants in Kentucky, Illinois, Oklahoma and Washington.

WILLIAM STEWART

December 9, 1839–December 11, 1907
Sangamon County, Illinois—Everett, Snohomish County, Washington

Grand Army of the Republic Cemetery
Everett, Snohomish County, Washington
Private, Company F, 29ᵗʰ Regiment, United States Colored Infantry
February 1, 1865–November 6, 1865
Chicago, Illinois—Brownsville, Texas

Company F, mainly consisting of Black men from Illinois and Missouri, did not meet the necessary quota of recruits. To supplement the ranks of soldiers, recruiting agents asked for men from Wisconsin, with larger bounties as enticements. Wisconsin's Black community was not large enough to fill the entire company. When the agents and company moved from Illinois to Virginia, the recruitment of other men from Virginia helped to fill the gap.

The *Chicago Tribune* played an active role in the raising of the Black Illinois regiment, the 29ᵗʰ U.S. Colored Infantry. On January 3, 1864, the paper insisted that the "colored people of the State owe it to themselves to fill up this regiment if possible before the month of January shall close" in order to "count so much against the impending draft." Taking a starkly practical turn, the paper argued that every man in the city of Chicago ought to be personally interested in filling the quota and so securing "himself from the chance of being drafted."[267]

U.S. Colored Troops military service records, 1863–65. *Image 1119, National Archive and Records Administration (NARA).*

For William Stewart, his decision to join the army came late in the war. He signed up in Chicago, Illinois, and received a bounty of $33.33 toward a total of $100. His transportation to Camp Butler in Springfield, Illinois, came nine days later. His enlistment papers described him as "age: twenty-five; occupation: farmer; eyes: black, hair: wooly; complexion: black; height five feet eleven inches."[268] In Camp Butler, he trained to become a soldier. Winter weather training caused many of the men to contract a multitude of diseases. Companies were losing men daily.

After wintering in Illinois, the regiment marched on March 27, 1865, south to join the

Army of the Potomac with the expectation of battling the Confederates. Stewart's commanding officer made the following statement:

> *About 1st day of March 1865 he* [William P. Stewart] *contracted diarrhea and was detailed as Mess Cook and excused from duty in the ranks as his disability was to such a degree as to make him unfit for active service and while at or near White Ranch, Texas he contract Rheumatism from which he has suffered ever since his discharge from the Army—Also at, or about the same time. March 1st, 1865, he contracted Pleurisy in his left side—from all of which diseases he has suffered since his discharge from the Army, and which has disqualified him from doing hard labor to earn a support for himself and family.*[269]

After successfully completing a small skirmish at Appomattox, the regiment moved to Petersburg, where it stayed for about a month—from the latter part of April to the first part of May. Orders came down to move the regiment to Texas via a steamer. With the treaty signed by Lee and Grant, the war was over, but the fighting continued in places where the news had not reached, including Texas.

In his pension records, William talked of the boat ride to Texas and getting very sick during the trip. The regiment was so large that it took two steamers: the *Wilmington* and the *William Kennedy*. The trip was anticipated to be a twelve-day voyage.

At the start of the journey, he was sick and became sicker as the voyage progressed. Battling diarrhea to start, he later developed pleurisy; this made his journey even more difficult. His brother-in-law, Aaron Roberts, in the same company and regiment, dictated a statement for Stewart's pension file on March 11, 1889:[270]

> [A]*bout April 20th, we embarked at Portsmouth via for Texas, he had been sick all the way down thair then whil at Whit Ranch Texas, he was taken with rheumatism from which he suffered more or less.*[271]

Stewart did not talk specifics about the trip to Texas, but in Edward Miller's book, *The Black Civil War Soldiers of Illinois*, part of the trip was described:

> *The ship carrying the Twenty-ninth Regiment and its brigade took on water and some provision at Fort Monroe and, with orders for Fort Morgan near Mobile, sailed on 27 May. The Kennedy reached Mobile*

Bay on 7 June, landing four companies at Navy Cove. Conditions ashore were poor—intense heat and swarms of stinging insects—so when the Wilmington arrived two days later with the rest of the regiment no one was put ashore, and the Kennedy's complement was anxious to go to sea again. Sailing on 9 and 10 June the flotilla took four days to reach Brazos de Santiago, Texas, but was unable to disembark the troops because of weather....[They] *finally landed at Brazos on June 22.*[272]

From the Brazos, the troops marched to Whites Ranch, about four miles from the mouth of the Rio Grande, and made camp. It was during this march that William claims to have contracted rheumatism.

William spent the balance of his enlistment in Texas under the command of W.E. Daggett. Upon mustering out in Brownsville, Texas, the regiment returned to Camp Butler in Springfield, Illinois, via steamer and finally was discharged from the army. At this point, the soldiers were allowed to purchase their weapon for $6.50, keep their canteen and knapsack and were given a small amount of money to defray the cost of traveling to their homes. William chose to return to Wisconsin.

William was born into a family whose history suggested they were free people of color and whose history extended as far back as 1730 to what is now Dinwiddie County, Virginia.[273] William's uncle, Dalton, made application to have his family declared Native American—it was his understanding that his grandparents on both sides of the family were Cherokee. To his regret, that application was denied in 1909. On the application, Dalton Stewart claimed that his father, Walden Stewart, was Choctaw and that his mother Polly Walden Stewart's grandmother was Cherokee.

William's family kept their residence in Morgan County, Illinois, from about 1835 until they moved to what is now Vernon County, Wisconsin, in 1855, where William's father, Walden Stewart, bought forty acres of land in 1857. They were part of small community called Cheyenne Valley consisting of free Blacks and some runaway slaves.[274]

In this small community, William may have known his future wife, Eliza Thornton, daughter of Abraham and Eleanor Carter Thornton. They married after William's return from the Civil War on October 25, 1868. Their only surviving child, Vey Stewart, was born in 1869.

For the next twenty years, William Stewart remained in Wisconsin, working the land. His physical health was deteriorating due to age, and the effects of the Civil War were also slowly weakening him. Additionally, rheumatism was

Left: Street sign of William P. Stewart Memorial Highway. *Author's collection.*

Right: William P. Stewart photograph, scanned from a photo of a larger group of men belonging to Grand Army of the Republic. *Displayed at Snohomish Cemetery Office.*

affecting his ability to farm his land and provide for his family. His pension records provided statements by him about his physical health and suffering: "[C]annot do manual labor on account of rheumatism, kidney complaint, catarrh of bladder, lung trouble and general debilities."[275] On the same application were the dates the diseases affected him: "[A]lleges contracted rheumatism in 1867, disease of kidney 1868, piles in 1881, malaria, bladder 1881, malaria lung trouble since 1886."

The Stewart family remained in Wisconsin until about 1889, when they appeared on the Washington Territorial census living in the Snohomish County area. Until his death in 1907, the family remained there. His son, Vey, married Eveline Green (also from the Cheyenne Valley community), and they had two children. Their second child, Maydrew, was the only surviving child. At an early age (thirteen or fourteen), she had lost both her parents in Washington, as recorded on the 1930 census for Snohomish County.

In 2002, several Snohomish County citizens approached the Washington State legislature to have a segment of a major highway in the state renamed for William P. Stewart. House Bill HJM 4024, dated 2002, was introduced to rename an 8.2-mile segment of Highway 99, aka Jefferson Davis Highway, to the William P. Stewart Highway. That bill was defeated. Instead, the highway was renamed Pioneer Highway. In a special session of the Washington State 64th legislature, House Joint Memorial 4010 was offered to rename Highway 99 to William P. Stewart Memorial Highway. The approved bill found its way to Governor Jay Inslee's desk and was signed in March 2016.

In an interview with his great-granddaughter M. Davis on February 13, 2010, more information was discovered about the family and their oral history as it was passed down, and she had her great-grandfather's photo album. She allowed pictures to be taken of those family photos.

William P. Stewart was interred at the Grand Army of the Republic Cemetery in Snohomish County, Washington, alongside his wife, Eliza, and Eliza's brother John.

He has living descendants in the state of Washington.

AFRICAN AMERICAN
CONFEDERATE PARTICIPANTS

Two African Americans participated in the war with the Confederates, according to their information on the 1910 census. These men, George Rawles and Nelson Carr, did not have pension files like the Union soldiers in this text. So, what you will get here is their family's history and any other information found.

GEORGE W. RAWLES

October 2, 1847–January 6, 1923
South Carolina—Seattle, King County, Washington
Mount Pleasant Cemetery, Seattle, Washington
Company B, 7th Battalion, Mississippi Infantry

George's journey to Washington State started with his birth in South Carolina to a noticeably young slave mother owned by Benjamin Rawles II.

At age seven and now living in Perry County, Mississippi, he was given to his master's son Benjamin Rawles III to be his body servant during the Civil War. Both enlisted in the Confederate army into Company B, 7th Battalion, Mississippi Infantry—Benjamin as an officer and George as a private. Although the battalion engaged in several battles—including the siege and surrender at Vicksburg, Mississippi, in May/June 1863 and the siege at

Atlanta, Georgia, in July/September 1864—it is not known if he actually took up arms against the Union army. Both he and his master survived the war. Benjamin died in 1910.

General Order No. 32 dated March 11, 1864 ("An Act to Increase the Efficiency of the Army by the Employment of Free Negroes and Slaves in Certain Capacities") may have been the reason George was used by the Confederate army. It states in part, "Whereas the efficiency of the army is greatly diminished by the withdrawal from the ranks of able-bodied soldiers to act as teamsters, and in various other capacities which free negroes and slaves might be advantageously employed."[276]

After the war, George returned to South Carolina with his first wife, Jane, and they became farmers. They had nine children, but only two survived to adulthood. When news of a mining boom in Lake County, Colorado, reached South Carolina in 1880, the family pulled up stakes and traveled to Leadville, Colorado, where George obtained a job as a "hod carrier." In Colorado, his wife passed away of heart failure, and he married the "Widow Jennie York."

With the dwindling of mining jobs after 1893, George and Jennie traveled to Seattle and found a house at 829 Northeast 67th Street. They stayed there for many years while George worked as an "on street laborer."

Oral history handed down to his descendants tells of their arrival into Seattle and one of them remarking that "the grass was green in August," so they stayed.

George's descendants are still living in Seattle.

NELSON CARR

Here is another African American man on the 1910 federal census who said that he took part in the "Confederate Army." There is no way to find out what part of the army he played a part in. He could have been taken in as a body servant or a laborer. If he had survived past 1924 and was still living in the South, he could have applied for a pension, but alas, he did not survive to 1924. He died on June 1, 1913, in Tacoma, Washington.

NOTES

Introduction

1. Civil War Trust, "Civil War Facts."
2. Former slaves had to prove cohabitations with spouses and provide "divorce decrees" for their separation from those cohabitations.
3. Prechtel-Kluskens, "Anatomy of a Union Civil War Pension File," 43.
4. A CD with Carper's pension file was mailed and received in July 2021.

Part I

5. General Affidavit, June 13, 1901, Roslyn, Kittitas County, Washington, National Archives and Records Administration; 8th Census of the United States, 1860, Slave Schedule, Series no. M653, Records of the Bureau of the Census, Record Group no. 2.
6. Wills, Probate, Madison County, 1833, John Amonet, via Ancestry.com.
7. Warren and Williams, *Donaldson Odyssey*, 47–48.
8. Thomas, Daniel, Jackson, Washington, found on the National Park Service website (https://www.nps.gov/civilwar/soldiers-and-sailors-database.htm) and Fold3 (https://www.fold3.com), T289, with Harry Donaldson identified as the father of Thomas.
9. Deposition, Donaldson, June 7, 1889, Marion County, Tennessee.
10. Smith, *Black Soldiers in Blue*, 221.
11. Disability Affidavit, Hamilton County, Tennessee, December 11, 1889.
12. General Affidavit, Jessee Donaldson, July 21, 1892.
13. Ibid.

14. General Affidavit, Jessee Donaldson, April 24, 1893.

15. *Cayton's Weekly*, "Colored News," 3.

16. *Letter of Expenses of U.S. v. Jessee Donaldson* to Edwin C. Miller Warden from R.M. Hopkins, Clerk, March 3, 1903.

17. Medical file, Jessee Donaldson, 2465, Veterans Affairs, Orting Soldiers Home, Member Files, 1891–1987, Washington State Archives, Digital Archives.

18. *Daily Illinois State Journal*, "Police Affairs," 4.

19. *Illinois Statewide Marriage Index*, "Marriage Records."

20. *Ellensburg Dawn*, "Alfred Paradise Died," 3.

21. *Ellensburg Capital*, "Death Comes to a Pioneer Colored Man," 3.

22. Cash receipt for services to be rendered, dated August 15, 1904.

23. Surgeon's Certificate, Ellensburg, Washington, November 23, 1904.

24. Washington, Kittitas County, Wills and Probate Records, 1,014.

25. *Daily Illinois Journal*, "R.H. Henson, Visiting Father, Frank Henson."

26. Arnold, "Fort Esperanza."

27. Norris, "Life During the Civil War, Fighting for Freedom," 40.

28. Chenery, *Fourteenth Regiment Rhode Island Heavy Artillery*, 62.

29. Ibid.

30. Ibid., 147.

31. This paragraph of the telegram was part of a larger article in the *Providence Evening Press* dated Wednesday, October 18, 1865, 2.

32. Deposition of Claimant, April 22, 1895, Peter B. Barrow, Pension File no. 821411, Civil War, Records Group 15, National Archives and Records Administration.

33. Ibid.

34. *Weekly Clarion*, "Radicals in Warren County," December 9, 1869, 2, col. 6.

35. Hauck, "Rev. Peter Barrow."

36. The Homestead Act of 1862, signed by Abraham Lincoln, allowed individuals to obtain 160 acres of public land for a nominal fee after five years of working and improving the land. If they could afford it, for $1.25 per acre, they could purchase the land outright ($200).

37. Bureau of Land Management, "Land Patent Search," General Land Office Records, http://www.glorecords.blm.gov/search/default.aspx.

38. *Spokane Press*, "Big Fruit Farm," 1.

39. *Seattle Republican*, Friday, October 4, 1907, 3, col. 2.

40. *Seattle Republican*, "Baptist Convention," 6.

41. *Tacoma Daily News*, "Injury Alone Not Fatal," 2.

42. *Spokane Press*, "Settled Minister's Death for $150," 1.

43. Deposition Bureau of Pensions, Charles James, November 11, 1907, Suffolk, Commonwealth of Massachusetts.

44. Charles in his pension file indicated that he worked for her when she was living on 14th Street in New York. Her address was verified through city directories online at Ancestry.com for the years 1876 and 1877. She was living at 317 West 14th Street.

45. Deposition, Alice James Freeman, November 12, 1926, Burlington, Vermont.

46. Letter of Agreement, February 8, 1905, *Charles James of Plymouth County, Massachusetts v. Martha James, and children of Burlington, Vermont.*
47. With the help of a staffer in Washington senator Maria Cantwell's office, I was put in touch with a governmental official responsible for approving Medal of Honors. I applied for a medal of honor for Scott. The application was declined for lack of witnesses to Scott's participation.
48. History of Claimants Disability, February 10, 1888, Rudolph Scott.
49. General Affidavit, January 2, 1896, taken in Spokane, Washington.
50. Claim for Pension, December 18, 1896, taken in Spokane, Washington.
51. Letter, B. Wilson, Office of the Chief Naval Operations Operation, Navy, Pentagon, Washington, D.C., to Mrs. Cynthia A. Wilson.
52. Franklin, *All Through the Night*, 20.
53. *Seattle Post-Intelligencer*, "Washington Pensions—Rudolph B. Scott Rejected," 2.
54. *Seattle Post-Intelligencer*, "Washington Pensions—Rudolph B. Scott," 2.
55. *Seattle Republican*, "Brothers in Black," 1.
56. *Seattle Daily Times Evening Edition*, "Rudolph B. Scott Removed," 9, col. 4.
57. Ibid., 21. Even though the newspaper suggests that Scott was part of Logan's unit, such was not the case.
58. Calarco et al., *Places of the Underground Railroad*, 31–32.
59. Lodwick, "Brown's County Civil War."
60. Helena, Montana City Directory noted that the family moved to Spokane.
61. Physician report, November 13, 1901, Spokane, Washington.
62. Letter, Mrs. Alice M. Scott, to "Dear Sir" Washington Gardner, Commissioner of Pensions, October 8, 1924.
63. Letter, Commissioner, Widow Division, to "Dear Madam" (Alice M. Scott), November 6, 1924.
64. Letter, E.L. Bailey, Director, Dependents Claims Service, to "My dear Mr. Coffee, Member of Congress," October 21, 1939.
65. During the research of the Abell family, there were several different spellings of the name: Abell, Abel and Able. For consistency, I will use the *Abell* spelling.
66. According to his enlistment papers, his owner, William M. Abell of Marion County, Kentucky, objected to his enlistment because he had not obtained permission to join.
67. Dobak and Phillips, *Black Regulars, 1866–1898*, 223.
68. Ibid., xii.
69. New Mexico State Register of Cultural Properties, "Application for Registration, For McRae."
70. All Civil War soldiers applying for pension were required to be examined by a rating board of three physicians to ascertain their physical health and to confirm their reported disabilities.
71. Letter, George Haswell, Special Examiner, to "Sir" Commissioner of Pensions, September 30, 1884, report of James Abell.
72. After her death, her granddaughter died a few days later. Seattle was in the midst of an exposition in 1901.

73. The area where the house was located is now Judkins Park, known as the "Central District" of Seattle, Washington.
74. "Pound master" was defined as a city's animal control person or local dog catcher. In 1923, the City of Seattle had five pound masters and four cars.
75. *Seattle Daily Times*, "Coyote Captured on Westlake Avenue," 3 and 13, respectively. Page 13 includes a picture of a captured coyote.
76. Deposition given by Jasper Evans to Pension Board, December 27, 1901.
77. Statement by Jasper Evans, March 28, 1899, taken in Bucoda, Washington.
78. *Evans v. Evans*, Divorce, City of St. Charles, Missouri, March 7, 1884, Block U, page 56, Circuit Court, St. Charles City, Missouri.
79. Bureau of Land Management, "Land Patent Search," General Land Office Records. Land was listed under the name "Jasper E. Jones."
80. Certificate of Medical Examination, Jasper Evans, claim no. 580022, Yakima, Washington.
81. Deposition of Edna V. Dale, MD, September 21, 1926, taken in Yakima County, Washington.
82. General Affidavit, taken in Yakima County, Washington, dated 1898.
83. *Seattle Republican*, November 3, 1905, 6.
84. Bryant Spencer identified his brother as John in a deposition dated October 9, 1885.
85. Deposition A, Spencer Jackson, Springfield, Ohio, October 9, 1885.
86. Ibid.
87. General Affidavit, deposition, John Spencer, Springfield, Ohio, December 10, 1892.
88. General Affidavit, Springfield, Ohio, April 28, 1891.
89. General Affidavit, Clark County, Ohio, December 15, 1916.
90. There had been some difficulty locating this family in 1900. The use of the Spencer name did not produce the family, but using the name of one of the children, the family was immediately located in Louisiana. Spencer Jackson was called by the name "Leslie R. Jackson," but all other members of the household had their correct names.
91. Bureau of Land Management, "Land Patent Search," General Land Office Records.
92. *Yakima Herald*, "Well Drilling Plants at Work."
93. Brodnax, "Will They Fight?," 282.
94. Ibid., 289.
95. Medical records obtained from the Museum of Colorado.
96. Brodnax, "Will They Fight?," 279.

Part II

97. He married under the name of Gideon Stump. Dodd, *Michigan Marriages*.
98. Welch, "Hot Work," 5–10.

99. *Seattle Post-Intelligencer*, "Constable Smalley's Luck," 5.

100. *Seattle Post-Intelligencer*, "Four Lives Are Lost," 5.

101. *Seattle Post-Intelligencer*, "They Died Despite Warnings," 2.

102. *Morning Olympian*, "Franklin Mine Victim," 4.

103. Mulcahy, "To Advance the Race," 62.

104. His headstone at the GAR cemetery acknowledges him as a "Grand Lecturer."

105. Since Gideon was married three times, Mary Elizabeth did not know about his first wife. His pension record only discusses the existence of two wives.

106. General Affidavit, Mary E. Bailey, August 1907, Seattle, King County, Washington, Pension no. 638576, Civil War, Records Group 15, National Archives and Records Administration.

107. *Mary Cook v. Norbin Cook.*

108. General Affidavit, Mary E. Bailey, July 28, 1906, Pension no. 638576, Civil War, Records Group 15, National Archives and Records Administration.

109. Retsil Soldiers Home, Mary Bailey, Patient no. 587-W.

110. Within this set of thirty soldiers, the other was Columbus Hollins.

111. Moss, *Forgotten Black Soldiers*.

112. This was a special edition published for the Alaska-Yukon-Pacific Exposition held in Seattle in 1909 on what is now the University of Washington campus.

113. Berwanger, *British Foreign Service*, 65.

114. Massachusetts, Suffolk County, 1870 U.S. census, population schedule, NARA microfilm publication M493, Roll 641, Page 455A, Image 272.

115. California, San Francisco County, 1880 U.S. census, Schedule for Defective, Dependent, and Delinquent Classes, Roll 97.6, Bancroft Library, University of California–Berkeley.

116. The building was constructed in 1889/1890 and demolished in 1957, making way for the Horton Building—still standing today.

117. *Seattle Republican*, "Joseph Benett," 4.

118. *Seattle Post-Intelligencer*, "Ancient York Masons Organize," 16, col. 1.

119. *Seattle Daily Times*, "Heart Attack Kills Woman," 3; *Seattle Daily Times*, "Obituary—Anna Bennett," 43.

120. Sworn statement by Joseph M. Bennett, May 5, 1932.

121. U.S. Public Health Service, "Clinical Record, History of Present Disease, Joseph P. Bennett."

122. U.S. Public Health Service, Marine Hospital, "Autopsy Report Joseph Bennett."

123. A "pioneer" is a soldier employed to perform engineering and construction tasks, as defined by Wikipedia.

124. Forstcher and Gingrich, "At Battle of the Crater."

125. Walter Scott has his own narrative.

126. Historic Sites of North Carolina, "Colored Troops at Fort Fisher."

127. *Seattle Daily Times*, "Henry Carper Get His Share; Retires, Shrewd Real Estate Dealer," 2.

128. Letter to John A. Smith, Esq., Clerk Circuit Court, D.C., May 20, 1862, signed by Barbara Williams, Washington, D.C., Slave Emancipation Records, 1851–

1863, National Archives and Records Administration (NARA), Records of the U.S. District Court for the District of Columbia Relating to Slaves, 1851–1863, Microfilm Serial: M433, Microfilm Roll 2, Record Group 21.

129. Deposition taken in Knoxville, Tennessee, on October 17, 1921, Mary J. Smith deposed.

130. *Knoxville Daily Chronicle*, "Notice, Henry Carper vs. Lucy Carper," 6.

131. *Knoxville Daily Journal*, "Sending Children to Ohio," 11.

132. *Knoxville Daily Tribune*, "Society Gossip, Last Week's Round of Gayeties," 4.

133. *Knoxville Journal*, "Boy Choir Concert."

134. *Semi-Weekly Knoxville Sentinel*, April 4, 1894, 4.

135. Declaration for Increase of Pension, Henry Carper, January 16, 1901.

136. "United States Veterans Administration Pension Payment Cards, 1907–1933."

137. *Seattle Daily Times*, "Henry Carper Gets His Share; Retires."

138. Ibid.; "Henry Carper Get His Share; Retires, Shrewd Real Estate Dealer," 13.

139. Corrections Department, Washington State Penitentiary, Commitment Registers and Mug Shots, 1887–1946, Washington State Archives, Digital Archives, http//digitalarchives.wa.gov.

140. *Seattle Daily Times*, "Master Burglar Stole for Drugs," 5.

141. *Seattle Star*, "Aged Father Bares Tragic Secret," 10.

142. *Seattle Daily Times*, "Old Soldiers to Teach Patriotism," May 21, 1916, 22.

143. *Memphis Daily Appeal*, August 15, 1882, image 2.

144. Case of Ella V. Carper, Certificate no. 1,162,556, dated June 1, 1921, Deposition A.

145. Cornish, *Sable Arm*, 75–76.

146. Ibid., 77.

147. Trudeau, *Like Men of War*, 6–7.

148. Urwin, *Black Flag Over Dixie*, 135.

149. Trudeau, *Like Men of War*, 193.

150. Statement of Facts, October 11, 1901, Department of the Interior, Bureau of Pensions.

151. Scurvy by medical definition is contracted from not eating foods rich in vitamin C (e.g., vegetables and organ meats).

152. Surgeon's Certificate, Medical Division, in the case of David Clark, January 20, 1895, medical evaluation by Dr. W.T. Wilson, Grays Lake, Idaho.

153. Deposition of I.L. Eastman of Soda Springs on July 28, 1898, Claim for Original Pension at Soda Springs, Bannock County, Idaho.

154. He used a variety of land acquisition programs: Homestead Act of 1862, Sale-Township, Settlement and Desert Land Act. Bureau of Land Management, "Land Patent Search," General Land Office Records.

155. Hospital Statement, April 8, 1895, Grays, Bingham City, Idaho.

156. "United States Veterans Administration Pension Payment Cards, 1907–1933."

157. *Oregonian*, "Portland Nurse Battling in Court," 14.

158. *Seattle Daily Times*, "Once Sold on Slave Block, He Pays Homage to Lincoln, February 12, 1930," 1 and 3.

159. Even though he stated that he was the only "colored member of GAR," he was not.
160. *Seattle Times*, "City Pays Tribute," February 12, 1930, 3.
161. *Morning Olympian*, "Negro Civil War Veteran," 1 and 8.
162. Ibid.
163. Ibid.
164. As of this year (2024), there is an error in his Civil War unit on his headstone; his middle initial and last name are also incorrect.
165. His name was spelled two ways: Donnegan and Donegan. There is a notation that John Donegan was not his real name, but that name was not noted.
166. James J. Donegan was in partnership with William Taber, Will Echols, George Beirne and Will Donegan in a company called Bell Factory Manufacturing Company. This company used what they called "Industrial Slaves" at a cost of thirty-five dollars per year for "manufacture of cotton and woolen yarns and… fabrics."
167. Wyeth, *Life of General Nathan Bedford Forrest*, 464.
168. Ibid.
169. *Union Army*, vol. 6, *History of Military Affairs in the Loyal States*, 53.
170. Berlin, Reidy and Rowland, *Freedom*, 591–92. Joseph did say that he managed to escape the enemy on December 7.
171. Letter, T.C. Ainsworth, Colonel, U.S. Army, Chief, Record and Pension Offices, to "Sir" Messer's A. Legg & Company.
172. This article was first published in the spring of 1991 in the *Sultana Remembered* newsletter, written and published by Pam Newhouse. The author of the article is the founder of the Sultana Association of Descendants and Friends, Norman Shaw.
173. Act of February 6, 1907, March 30, 1907.
174. Letter from Julie Donegan, "Dear Sir" Commissioner of Pension, December 17, 1925.
175. Brown, Textual Reference Operations, National Archives at College Park, Maryland, to "Dear Ms. Wilson," May 11, 2022.
176. Letter (e-mail), St. Louis Archives, NARA. Here are the databases suggested for searching: http://www.ancestry.com, http://go.fold3.com, https://www.familysearch.org/search/collection/2968245 or http://www. heritagequestonline.com/hqoweb/library/do/index. A subscription fee may be required. You may also view these records online for free at any NARA location using ALIC or a public access PC. All NARA locations are listed at http://www.archives.gov/locations.
177. Ancestry.com, Freedmen's Bureau Marriage Records, 1815–1866.
178. Smith, *Black Soldiers in Blue*, 221.
179. Clark worked on the *War Eagle* from the end of 1869 to early 1870. The *War Eagle* was a side-wheel riverboat built in Ohio in 1854. Clark, hired by George M. Dunsberry, worked on the *Damsel* in the summer of 1870. The *Damsel* sank on April 3, 1873, in the rapids above Keokuk, Iowa.
180. Ross was born 1894 in Wisconsin, while the assumed father, Clark, was living in Minnesota.

181. *St. Paul Globe*, "Clark Harris Free," 2.

182. *La Crosse (WI) Tribune*, "Mrs. Maud Harries Dies," 1.

183. *St. Paul Daily Globe*, "Salvation Army Morals," 2.

184. Andrew Raymond Black was an up-and-coming African American lawyer from Virginia. Just after graduating from Howard University of Washington, D.C., he moved to Seattle in about 1902 and became a partner with J.E. Hawkins for a while before striking out on his own. His caseload included real estate, divorces and helping Civil War soldiers and their widows with processing pension applications (1861–1907).

185. Letter, Andrew R. Black, to "Gentlemen," Department of the Interior," August 12, 1911.

186. Ibid.

187. Ibid., August 30, 1911.

188. Ibid., November 24, 1911.

189. Ibid., May 12, 1912.

190. Stillwell, Acting Commission, to "Sir" Andrew R. Black, September 6, 1912. It seems that Mr. Black was just a notary public on many of the applications that Elizabeth signed. Elizabeth hired W.H. Wills as her true attorney on January 25, 1913, to represent her to the pension bureau.

191. Washington, King County, Wills and Probate Records, Case no. 13130, Box 594a, 13,127–13,131, 1911.

192. She had her 103rd birthday in April 2024.

193. Deposition, case of Gilford Hervey, January 29, 1896, taken in North Indianapolis, Marion County, Indiana.

194. Humphreys, *Intensely Human*, 27.

195. Wyeth, *Life of General Nathan Bedford Forrest*, 397.

196. Deposition taken on January 29, 1876, North Indianapolis, Indiana.

197. Bureau of Land Management, "Land Patent Search," General Land Office Records.

198. John C. Black to "Dear Sir" Bureau of Pensions, November 26, 1888.

199. Using a letter in Gilford's pension file, I located her living in Milwaukee, Wisconsin, with her husband, John. She was born in Kansas in about 1895 to parents Phillip and Jane Gill Hervey. Gilford Hervey was not her father.

200. *The Freeman*, "New Church Organized."

201. *Yakima Herald*, "Colony Is Planned."

202. According to a letter dated October 22, 1920, from Superintendent of Mails G.E. Williams, the last day Gilford picked up his mail was September 3. Actually, a transcription of his patient record indicated an e-mail from Sarah Nelson Smith, Archivist Librarian, December 24, 2014. In July 2023, a digital image of the logbooks of deaths was released under the auspices of the *Seattle Times*. It confirms Hervey's stay and death in the Northern State Hospital.

203. This was part of a package of documents related to the probating of his estate by Ella M. Brown—in the possession of the author.

204. He was in Sedro Woolley at the time. Carey Hervey to "Dear Sir" Commissioner of Pension, September 5, 1922.

205. Ibid.
206. Guy Taylor, Disbursing Clerk, to "Dear Chief, Finance Division of the Pension Office" and to "Dear Carey Hervey," October 28, 1920.
207. Iwasaki, "Women's Genealogy Search," B1, 5.
208. "U.S. City Directories, 1821–1989," Portland, Oregon, via Ancestry.com.
209. *Oregonian*, "Courts," 3.
210. Orting Soldiers Home, Orting, Washington, Medical File no. 1194, Veterans Affairs, Member Files, 1891–1987, Washington State Archives, Digital Archives.
211. Deposition A, page 2, July 2, 1887, Guthrie, Logan County, Oklahoma Territory.
212. *Finding Your Roots*, Season 7, Episode 5, "Write My Name in the Book of Life."
213. Handwritten interview notes described the locations but not the names of four colored schools in Galesburg. Information taken from an interview of J. Howell Atwood with John Bell and J.J. Brown during the years 1930–60, J. Howell Atwood Manuscript Collection, Box 8, Knox College, Illinois.
214. Knox College Library, Special Collections and Archives, http://www.library.knox.edu/archives/exhibits/blacks/citydirectories.htm#1857.
215. Cities described by him were Fairburg, Decatur, Valentine and Omaha.
216. Brief and Argument in the matter of Appeal of Claimant Invalid C'l'f' no. 691,494 of Augustus Dixon, Company E, 60th Regiment, U.S.C. Infantry, page 3, attorney R.A Grossman.
217. Affidavit of William C. Phillips for Augustus Dixon, Washington State, Pierce County, May 19, 1908.
218. Affidavit of Belle Evans for Augustus Dixon, State of Washington, County of Yakima, May 19, 1903.
219. Notorized statement by Belle Evans for Augustus Dixon dated May 19, 1903, in Yakima County, Washington, found in Dixon's pension file.
220. "U.S. Veterans Administration Pension Payment Cards, 1907–33, via https://familysearch.org.
221. Sworn statement given by Columbus Hollins, Washington State, Pierce County, May 26, 1914.
222. *Minnesota, Civil War Records, 1861–1865*, via Ancestry.com.
223. *Minnesota Historical Society Press* 1, "Narrative of the First Battery of Light Artillery."
224. National Archives and Records Administration, "Returns from Regular Army Cavalry Regiments."
225. Hill, "Exploring the Life and History."
226. Deposition, November 23, 1908, Camp Nelson.
227. Sutherland, *African Americans at War*, 81.
228. Squire, "24th Infantry Regiment and the Racial Debate," 37.
229. National Archives and Records Administration, "U.S. Customs Services."
230. *San Francisco Examiner*, "'Bowhead' Loss," 3.
231. *U.S. Customs Services, Records of the U.S. Coast Guard*, Shipping Articles and Crew Lists, 1851–1950, Record Group 26.
232. A copy of Samuel Johnson's King County probate record was found at the Puget Sound Archives on the campus of Bellevue Community College in Bellevue, Washington.

233. Deposition, July 10, 1901, taken at Orting, Pierce County, Washington.
234. Will is dated March 20, 1851. Kentucky Wills, researched by Hightfield.
235. Even though Samuel stated that his brother died in Wilson Hospital, my research found that his brother James spent the next thirty-four years in the U.S. Army and applied for a pension on February 20, 1900, in Arizona. He served, after the war, in the 10th Cavalry (Company I), 41st U.S. Infantry (Company D), 24th U.S. Infantry (Company C and D), 24th U.S. Infantry (Company K) and General Mtd Services.
236. Physician Certificate, May 22, 1901.
237. Physician's Affidavit, February 27, 1906.
238. Larkins to "Gentlemen," Hon Board of Control, Olympia, Washington, October 25, 1907.
239. Young and Bogumill, *Comprehensive History of the Washington Soldiers' Home and Colony*, 10.
240. Legislator J.C. Taylor proposed that "veterans with families move into housing within the City of Orting. The whole family would then receive medical care. The federal government would pay its share of the expenses by paying the state $100.00 a year, per home resident." The state legislature accepted this proposal.
241. Patient file C492, Miriam Young, Colony at Soldier's Home, 8.
242. Trudeau, *Like Men of War*, 343.
243. Deposition A, Case of David Slaughter, No. 840 827, August 2, 1892, Indianapolis, Indiana.
244. Muster Rolls of Company F, 114th U.S. Colored Infantry, March–April 1865, 1784–1912, Records Group 94, M594, National Archives and Records Administration, Pacific Region, Seattle, Washington.
245. Christian, "Fort Ringgold."
246. Humphreys, *Intensely Human*, 27.
247. Invalid Pension, Muncie, Indiana, April 23, 1901.
248. Deposition A, David Slaughter, August 2, 1892, Indianapolis, Marion County, Indiana.
249. Invalid Pension, Muncie, Indiana, April 23, 1901.
250. Ibid.
251. Letter from David T. Slaughter to "Dear Friends," U.S. Department of Pension for War Veterans, December 11, 1928.
252. Letter from Winfred Scott to David T. Slaughter, "Dear Sir," February 12, 1929.
253. Muster Roll for Company K, March and April 1865, confirmed that he was in Charleston, South Carolina. M594, "Compiled Records Showing Service of Military Units."
254. Indianapolis City Directories, 1883–85.
255. *The Appeal*, "Doings In and About the Great 'Flour City,'" 3, col. 6.
256. Ibid.
257. Deposition A, Atha Hunter, August 11, 1901, Boonville, Warrick County, Indiana.
258. Deposition A, Newton B. Plummer, September 4, 1903, Belknap, New Hampshire.

259. Letter, Chief of Law Division, to "Sir" Chief of the S.E. Division of Bureau of Pensions, December 2, 1903.

260. It is assumed that Alfred cohabitated with Sarah since marriage among slaves was not "lawful." Sarah died on December 12, 1857.

261. Wills, 1796–1935, Bullitt County, Kentucky, LDS Family History Library, Microfilm, Kentucky Probate Records, 1727–1990, Books E/F, Film no. 482686, via http://familysearch.org.

262. Glatthaar, *Forged in Battle*, 124.

263. Weldman, "Fight for Equal Rights."

264. Deposition taken by R. Maxton, Clerk of the Court, for the County of McLean, Illinois, October 29, 1888, Alfred Samuels Civil War Pension File.

265. Deposition given by Dr. W.C. Cox, April 24, 1903.

266. Surgeon's Deposition by Dr. W.C. Cox, June 20, 1903.

267. Cornish, *Sable Arm*, 250.

268. Other documents within his pension file note a height of five feet, six inches.

269. Invalid Claim for Pension, August 8, 1887, by William P. Stewart, Marionette County, Wisconsin.

270. Aaron Roberts was the spouse of William Stewart's sister, Martha Stewart.

271. Deposition given by Aaron Roberts, March 11, 1889.

272. Miller, *Black Civil War Soldiers of Illinois*, 156.

273. Heinegg, *Free Blacks of North Carolina and Virginia*.

274. Cooper, *Black Settlers in Rural Wisconsin*.

275. Original Invalid Claimant, August 24, 1901. On this document, his application was rejected on February 14, 1902.

276. Moebs, *Black Soldiers, Black Sailors, Black Ink*, 1,349.

Bibliography

Aberdeen Herald. "Nominations to Office." October 27, 1892, 4.

The Appeal (St. Paul, MN). "Doings In and About the Great 'Flour City.'" March 19, 1904, 3.

———. "Marriage Announcement." March 19, 1904, 3.

———. "R.B. Scott Passes Thru." August 16, 1890, 2.

———. "Spokane Falls, Wash." July 26, 1890, 1.

Application for Registration, New Mexico State Register of Cultural Properties, Property Number 1826, Fort McRae. http://www.newmexicohistory.org/uploads/9969/Ft.%20McRae%20SR%20Nomination.pdf.

Arkansas Mansion. "Personal—Baptist Sabbath School Convention." August 25, 1883, 4.

Arnold, J. Barto, III. "Fort Esperanza." Handbook of Texas Online, January 1, 1995. http://www.tshaonline.org/handbook/online/articles/qcf02.

Barrow, Charles Kelly, and J.H. Seagars, eds. *Black Southerners in Confederate Armies: A Collection of Historical Accounts.* Gretna, LA: Pelican Publishing, 2001.

Berlin, Ira, Joseph P. Reidy and Leslie S. Rowland. *Freedom: A Documentary of History of Emancipation, 1861–1867.* Series 2, *The Black Military Experience.* Cambridge, MA: Cambridge University Press, 1982.

Berwanger, Eugene H. *The British Foreign Service and the American Civil War.* Lexington: University Press Kentucky, 1994.

Blackett, R.J.M., ed. *Thomas Morris Chester: Black Civil War Correspondent—His Dispatches from the Virginia Front.* Baton Rouge: Louisiana State University Press, 1989.

Boston Daily Advertiser. "USS *Chicopee,*" June 9, 1864, 4.

Brodnax, David, Sr. "Will They Fight? Ask the Enemy: Iowa's African American Regiment in the Civil War." *Annals of Iowa* (2007): 279, 282, 289.

Brown, John Bell, and J.J. Brown. Interview by J. Howell Atwood. J. Howell Atwood Manuscript Collection, Box 8, Knox College, Illinois, 1930–60.

Burt, Terr. "Leaky Barrels Fueled Blaze on War Eagle." *La Crosse Tribune*, April 17, 1990, A12.

Bush, F.N. Additional notes to Certificate of Medical Examination. Maryland, December 16, 1926.

Calarco, Tom, with Cynthia Vogel, Kathryn Grover, Rae Hallstrom, Sharron Pope and Melissa Waddy-Thibodeaux. *Places of the Underground Railroad: A Geographical Guide.* Santa Barbara, CA: ABC-CLIO, 2011.

Cartmell, Donald. *The Civil War Up Close.* United States: Career Press Inc., 2005.

Cayton's Weekly. "Colored News." March 29, 1919, 3.

Chenery, William H. *The Fourteenth Regiment Rhode Island Heavey Artillery (Colored) in the War to Preserve the Union, 1861–1865.* Providence, RI: Snow & Farnham, 1898.

Christ, Mark K., ed. *All Cut to Pieces and Gone to Hell: The Civil War, Race Relations, and the Battle of Spring.* Little Rock, AR: August House Publishers Inc., 2003.

Christian, Garna L. "Fort Ringgold." Handbook of Texas Online, October 22, 2010. https://www.tshaonline.org/handbook/entries/fort-ringgold.

Civil War Helena. "This Is the Story of Our Nation's Struggle." U.S. Colored Troops in Helena. http://civilwarhelena.com/history/us-colored-troops.

Civil War Pension Index. "General Index to Pension Files, 1861–1934." 2007. http://ancestry.com.

Civil War Times. "Commemorating CSS Albemarle's Sinking." February (2015): 14.

Civil War Trust. "Civil War Facts: Saving American's Civil War Battlefields." http://www.civilwar.org/education/history/faq.

Cleveland Morning Leader. "Bravery of the Negro Troops." September 5, 1864, 3.

Coddington, Ronald S. *African American Faces of the Civil War: An Album.* Baltimore, MD: Johns Hopkins University Press, 2012.

Colorado Statesman. "Rudolph B. Scott." April 10, 1909, 5.

Columbia Courier (Kennewick, WS). "Fort Sherman National Soldier's Home." September 4, 1903, 2.

Colville Examiner. "Notice of Private Sale of Real Estate." November 14, 1908, 4.

———. "Notice of Public Sale of Real Estate." October 9, 1909, 7.

———. "Notice of Public Sale of Real Estate." October 2, 1909, 3.

"Compiled Records Showing Service of Military Units in Volunteer Union Organizations." Microfilm Publication M594, 225 rolls. Washington, D.C.: National Archives and Records Administration, 1965.

Cook, Rebecca. "Article: House Willing to Ditch Jeff Davis—Highway Honoring Rebel Leader Would Be Named for Black Union Soldier." *Yakima Herald-Republic*, February 16, 2002.

Cooper, Zachary. *Black Settlers in Rural Wisconsin.* Madison: State Historical Society of Wisconsin, 1994.

Cornish, Dudley Taylor. *The Sable Arm: Black Troops in the Union Army, 1861–1865.* Lawrence: University Press of Kansas, 1987.

Daily Commerical (Vicksburg). "Circuit Court." June 3, 1878.

———. "Colored Voters and Republicans." November 3, 1879, 2.

———. "The Newtown Picnic." June 27, 1879, 4.

———. "The Vote of Warran County." November 7, 1879, 4.

Daily Illinois Journal (Springfield). "R.H. Henson, Visiting Father, Frank Henson." 1916.

Daily Illinois State Journal. (Springfield). "Police Affairs." 1873.

Declaration for Increase of Pension. Henry Carper, January 16, 1901, Knoxville, Tennessee.

Department of Veterans Affairs."Civil War and Later Pension Files." Record Group 15, National Archives and Records Administration, Washington, D.C.

Dobak, William A. *Freedom by the Sword: The U.S. Colored Troops, 1862–1867*. New York: Skyhorse Publishing Inc., 2013.

Dobak, William A., and Thomas D. Phillips. *The Black Regulars, 1866–1898*. Norman: University of Oklahoma Press, 2001.

Dodd, Jordan, of Liahona Research, comp. *Michigan Marriages, 1851–1875*. Provo, UT: Ancestry.com Operations Inc., 2000.

Durham, Nelson Wayne. *History of the City of Spokane and Spokane County Washington from Its Earliest Settlement to the Present Time*. Spokane, WA: S.J. Clarke Publishing Company, 1912.

Ellensburg Capital. "Death Comes to Pioneer Colored Man—Frank Henson." January 11, 1917, 3.

Ellensburg Dawn. "Alfred Paradise Died." November 20, 1913, 3.

Evening Statesman (Walla Walla, WA). "Back to China." December 12, 1904, 1.

———. "James Barrow Seeks Pardon." July 14, 1905, 5.

Everett Daily Herald. "Obituary—Cicero Hunter." May 12, 1916.

Everett Evening Records. "Obituary—Alfred Samuels." October 7, 1906.

Farbar, Greg. "Black Civil War Veteran Buried Here." *Issaquah Press*, December 31, 2008, B4.

Faust, Drew Gilpin. *This Republic of Suffering: Death and the American Civil War*. New York: Vintage Books, 2008.

Forstcher, William, and Newt Gingrich. "At Battle of the Crater, Black Troops Proved Their Courage." *Washington Post*, 2014.

Franklin, John Hope, and Alfred A. Moss Jr. *From Slavery to Freedom*. 6th ed. New York: McGraw-Hill Inc., 1988.

Franklin, Joseph M. *All Through the Night: The History of Spokane Black Americans, 1860–1940*. Spokane, WA: Ye Gallon Press, 1989.

"Freedman's Bank Records, 1865–1874." Database and Images, 2007. http://www.ancestry.com.

The Freeman (Indianapolis, IN). "Bishop Grant's Address." August 27, 1910, 3.

———. "New Church Organized." July 13, 1895.

Glatthaar, Joseph T. *Forged in Battle: The Civil War Alliance of Black Soldiers and White Officers*. Baton Rouge: Louisiana State University Press, 1990.

Gould, William B., IV. *Diary of a Contraband: The Civil War Passage of a Black Sailor*. Stanford, CA: Stanford University Press, 2002.

Gourdin, John R. *Borrowed Identity: 128th United Stated Colored Troops—Multiple Named Usage by Black Civil War Veterans Who Served with Union Regiments Organized in South Carolina*. Westminster, MD: Heritage Books, 2009.

Gourdin, John Raymond. *The Book of First, Last, Etcetera: Black Soldiers during the Civil War Era, 1861–1867.* Columbia, MD: J&M Publishing, 2003.

Greenberg, Martin H., and Charles G.Waugh, eds. *The Price of Freedom: Slavery and the Civil War.* Nashville, TN: Cumberland House Publishing, 2000.

Greene, A. "Weldon Railroad, Battle of the." *Encyclopedia Virginia.* N.p.: Virginia Humanities, 2021.

Groene, Bertram Hawthorne. *Tracing Your Civil War Ancestor.* New York: John F. Blair, 1973.

Gutman, Herbert G. *The Black Family in Slavery and Freedom, 1750–1925.* New York: Vintage Books, 1976.

Hargrove, Hondon B. *Black Union Soldiers in the Civil War.* Jefferson, NC: McFarland & Company Inc., Publishers, 1988.

Hauck, Janet. "Rev. Peter Barrow (1840–1906)." BlackPast. http://www.blackpast.org.

"Headstone Applications, 1909–1962, Memorial Division, Records of the Quartermaster General's Office, Record Group 92." Washington, D.C.: National Archives and Records Administration (NARA), n.d.

Heinegg, Paul. *Free Blacks of North Carolina and Virginia.* Baltimore, MD: Clearfield Company Genealogical Publishing Company, 2005.

Hesseltine, William B., ed. *Civil War Prisons.* Kent, OH: Kent State University Press, 1962.

Hill, Walter. "Exploring the Life and History of the 'Buffalo Soldiers.'" *The Record: National Archives and Records Administration (NARA).* March 1998. http://www.archives.gov/publications/record/1998/03/buffalo-soldiers.html.

Historic Sites of North Carolina. "Colored Troops at Fort Fisher." https://historicsites.nc.gov/all-sites/fort-fisher/history/civil-war-ft-fisher/2nd-attack/colored-troops-fort-fisher.

Holmes, E.H. "The Far Northwest: Land Where Prejudice Is a Minimum and Where Prosperity Awaits All Thrifty Sons of Africa." *Freeman Indianapolis,* August 15, 1891, 6.

Horwitz, Tony. "PTSD: The Civil War's Hidden Legacy." *The Smithsonian* (January 2015): 44–49.

Humphreys, Margaret. *Intensely Human: The Health of the Black Soldier in the American Civil War.* Baltimore, MD: Johns Hopkins University Press, 2010.

Idaho Register. "Cancellation of Taxes." January 6, 1914, 7.

Illinois Statewide Marriage Index, 1796–1900. "Marriage Records." Illinois State Archives.

"Index to Pension Applications Files of Remarried Widows Based on Service in the Civil War and Later Wars and in the Regular Army after the Civil War." Microfilm publication M1785. Washington, D.C.: National Archives and Records Administration (NARA), 1993.

Issaquah/Sammamish Reporter. "The Grand Army of the Republic Comes to Issaquah." March 25, 2014.

Iwasaki, John. "Women's Genealogy Search Yields Enormous Discovery." *Seattle Post-Intelligencer,* March 5, 2004, B1, B5.

Jefferson, Baba Ashanti. "Black Roots Deep, Worth Attention." *Spokesman-Review*, February 23, 1997, 1.

Jordan, Ervin L., Jr. *Black Confederates and Afro-Yankees in Civil War Virginia*. Charlottesville: University Press of Virginia, 1995.

Judd, Ron. "Bring Out Your Dead: In Recording Who's Buried Where, History Comes Alive." *Seattle Times*, October 26, 2012, 25.

Kansas City Sun. "The Golden West: The Colored American Making Good in the Far West and a Steady Stream of Desirable Immigrants New Pouring into that Spendid County with the Wonderful Possibilities." February 5, 1916, 1.

Kentucky Wills. Researched by Vikki Hollowell Hightfield. Ancestry. http://freepages.genealogy.rootsweb.ancestry.com/~hollowel/index.html.

Killian, Crawford. *Go Do Some Great Thing: The Black Pioneers of British Columbia*. Burnaby, BC: Commodore Books, 2008.

Kittitas County Centennial Committee. *Kittitas County, Washington, 1989*. Dallas, TX: Taylor Publishing Company, 1989.

Knox College Library. "Blacks in Galesburg: City Directory Information." 1857, 1861 and 1867. http://www.library.knox.edu/archives/exhibits/blacks/citydirectories.htm#1857.

Knoxville Daily Chronicle. "Church Program." January 1, 1882, 5. GenealogyBank.com.

———. "Henry Carper's New Residence." May 9, 1882, 6. Chronicling America, Library of Congress, Online Archives.

———. "Notice, Henry Carper vs. Lucy Carper." January 7, 1866, 6.

———. "The Youthful Thieves." January 1, 1882, 5. GenealogyBank.com.

Knoxville Daily Journal. "Runaway." March 18, 1873, 4. Chronicling America, Library of Congress, Online Archives.

———. "Sending Children to Ohio." January 3, 1886, 11.

Knoxville Daily Tribune. "Court Transacted." February 22, 1878, 4. GenealogyBank.com.

———. "Society Gossip, Last Week's Round of Gayeties: How Knoxville People Are Enjoying Themselves—Receptions and Social Parties and Who Attended Them." March 20, 1887, 4.

Knoxville Journal. "The Boy Choir Concert." May 13, 1892.

Knoxville Weekly Chronicle. "Chancery Court at Knoxville, Tenn." March 19, 1873, 6. Chronicling America, Library of Congress, Online Archives.

———. "Church Program." April 20, 1870, 6. GenealogyBank.com.

Knoxville Whig and Chronicle. "Advertised Letters." August 11, 1875, 2. GenealogyBank.com.

La Crosse Leader Press. "Death of Mrs. Maud Harris." September 28, 1907, 7.

La Crosse (WI) Tribune. "Funeral—Maud Harris." September 30, 1907, 1.

———. "Mrs. Maud Harris Dies." September 28, 1907, 1.

Lardas, Mark. *African American Soldier in the Civil War*. Great Britian: Osprey Publishing Ltd., 2006.

Lewis, Oscar. *The War in the Far West, 1861–1865: An Informal History of the Part Played by the Western States in the Civil War*. Garden City, NY: Doubleday & Company Inc., 1961.

Livingston, Jill. "The Jefferson Davis Highway Out West." *Living Gold Press*, February 2007.

Lodwick, Ned. "Brown's County Civil War." Article 18. Brown County Department of Travel & Tourism.

Mary Cook v. Norbin Cook. Divorce Decree, May 8, 1876. Peoria, IL. Located in pension file.

McPherson, James M. *For Cause & Comrades: Why Men Fought in the Civil War*. Oxford, UK: Oxford University Press Inc., 1997.

————. Introduction and Notes. *The Most Fearful Ordeal: Original Coverage of the Civil War*. New York: New York Times Company, 2004.

————. *The Negro's Civl War: How American Blacks Felt and Acted During the War for the Union*. New York: Anchor Books, 1993.

Memphis Daily Appeal. August 15, 1882, image 2.

"Michigan Marriages, 1851–1875." 2000. http://www.ancestry.com.

"Military, Compiled Service Records, Civil War. Carded Records, Volunteer Organizations." *Records of the Adjutant General's Office, 1780–1917, Record Group 94*. Washington, D.C.: National Archives and Records Administration (NARA).

Miller, Edward A., Jr. *The Black Civil War Soldiers of Illinois: The Story of the Twenty-Ninth U.S. Colored Infantry*. Columbia: University of South Carolina Press, 1998.

Miller, Ilanda D. *Report from America: William Howard Russell and the Civil War*. Great Britian: Simon Publishing Limited, 2001.

Minneapolis Journal. "Town Talk." December 11, 1900, 7.

Minnesota, Civil War Records, 1861–1865, via Ancestry.com. Original, *Minnesota Civil War Muster Rolls*. St. Paul: Minnesota Historical Society, 2011.

Minnesota Historical Society Press 1. "Narrative of the First Battery of Light Artillery, Minnesota in the Civil and Indian Wars" (2005): 658.

Moebs, Thomas. *Black Soldiers, Black Sailors, Black Ink: Research Guide on African Americans in U.S. Military History, 1526–1900*. N.p.: Moebs Publishing Company, 1994.

Morning Olympian. "Edward Clark." February 13, 1930, 1.

————. "Franklin Mine Victim: Bones of the Men Killed Last October Identified." December 12, 1895, 4.

————. "Negro Civil War Veteran Relates High Adventures." June 24, 1932, 1 and 8.

Morris, Scott. "It Wasn't Easy Being Different—Siblings of One of the Few Early Black Families in Arlington Fondly Recall Their Upbringing, but Also Recall a Constant Undercurrent of Racism." *The Herald* (Everett, WA), September 19, 2004.

Moss, Juanita D. *The Forgotten Black Soldiers in White Regiments During the Civil War*. N.p.: Heritage Books, 2008.

Mulcahy, Richard P., PhD. "To Advance the Race: Prince Hall Freemasonry and the Founding of the Niagara Movement." *Hibiscus Masonic Review* 3 (2009–10): 62.

Mumford, Esther Hall. *Seattle's Black Victorians, 1852–1901*. Seattle, WA: Ananse Press, 1980.

National Archives and Records Administration. "Compiled Record Showing Service of Military Units in Volunteer Union Organizations M594." 1965.

———. "Muster Rolls of Regular Army Organizations, 1784–1912." Records of the Adjutant General's Office, 1780s–1917, Record Group 94. Washington, D.C.

———. "Returns from Regular Army Cavalry Regiments, 1833–1916." M744-95. Pacific Alaska Region, Seattle, Washington.

———. *U.S. Civil War Pension Index: General Index to Pension Files, 1861–1934.*

———. "U.S. Customs Services." Records of the Adjutant General Office, Copies of Wreck Report, 1874–1943.

National Park Service. "Civil War Soldiers and Sailors System." 2007. http://www.itd.nps.gov/cwss.

National Tribune. "The Address of G.P. Hervey." May 6, 1909, 8.

"Nat Turner Lodge No. 2." October 19, 1889, 4. Periodical unknown.

Naval Historical Center. "Dictionary of American Naval Fighting Ships." Washington Navy Yard, Washington, D.C. http://www.history.navy.mil/danfs/p10/potomska.htm.

New Haven Register. "Business on the Pacific Coast: Rudolph V. Scott Talks of the Rust to Alaska's Great Fields." May 24, 1897, 1.

Newman, Debra L. *Black History: A Guide to Civilian Records in the National Archives.* Washington, D.C.: National Archives Trust Fund Board, General Services Administration, 1984.

New Mexico State Register of Cultural Properties. "Application for Registration, For McRae."

Norris, David. "Life During the Civil War, Fighting for Freedom: The U.S. Colored Troops." *Moorhead Magazine* (2009): 40.

Norvell, Scott. "Road Rage—Jefferson Davis Highway." January 28, 2002. FoxNews.com.

O'Connor, Bob. *The U.S. Colored Troops at Andersonville Prison.* N.p.: Infinity Publishing, 2009.

Olson, Cory, and Diane Olson. *Black Diamond: Mining the Memories.* Black Diamond, WA: Black Diamond Historical Society, 2003.

Oregonian. "Courts—John Christopher." September 9, 1873, 3.

———. "Death in the Mines: Terrible Accident at the Franklin Collier. Thirty-Seven Miners Are Killed." August 25, 1894, 1–2.

———. "The Horror of Franklin: Local Agent of the O.I. Co. Talks of the Disaster." August 26, 1894, 16.

———. "Portland Nurse Battling in Court for $250,00 Claimed from RCA Stock Transaction." May 12, 1964, 14.

———. "RCA Stock Ruling Ok'd." December 29, 1964, 28.

Paradis, James M. *Strike the Blow for Freedom: The 6th United States Colored Infantry in the Civil War.* Shippenburg, PA: White Mane Publishing, 2000.

Pettit, Steafanie. "Church Founder and Activist Arrived in 1889." *Spokesman-Review,* December 23, 2010, 1.

Portland Skanner. "Washington Highway Prompts Hate Mail." February 13, 2002.

Prechtel-Kluskens, Claire. "Anatomy of a Union Civil War Pension File." *Newsmagazine* 34, no. 3 (July–September 2008).

Providence Evening Press. "Return of the Eleventh Colored Regiment." October 1865, 1865, 2.

Puget Sound Archives, Bellevue Community College Campus. Probate Records for Samuel Johnson.

Pullman Herald (Pullman, Washington Territory). "Were Granted Pensions—Rudolph B. Scott." September 25, 1897, 2.

Quarles, Benjamin. *The Negro in the Civil War.* New York: Da Capo Press Inc., 1953.

Ramold, Steven J. *Slaves, Sailors, Citizens: African Americans in the Union Army.* DeKalb: Northern Illinois University Press, 2002.

Records of the Adjutant General's Office. 1780s–1917. *Field and Staff Muster Roll Report.* Record Group 94, National Archives and Records Administration.

Records of the U.S. District Court for the District of Columbia Relating to Slaves, 1851–63. Letter to John A. Smith, Esq., Clerk Circuit Court, D.C., May 20, 1862, signed by Barbara Williams. NARA.

Redkey, Edwin S., ed. *A Grand Army of Black Men.* Cambridge, MA: Cambridge University Press, 1992.

"Register of Enlistments in the United States Army, 1798–1914." Microfilm publication M233, 81 rolls. National Archives and Records Administration, 1956.

"Register of Signatures of Depositors in Branches of the Freedmen Savings and Trust Company, 1805–1874." Microfilm Publication M816, 27 rolls. National Archives and Records Administration, 1970.

Rein, Christopher M. *Alabamians in Blue, Freedmen, Unionists, and the Civil war in the Cotton State.* Baton Rouge: Louisiana State University Press, 2019.

Retsil Soldiers Home. Mary Bailey, Patient no. 587-W. Bremerton, Washington. Digital image, Washington State Digital Archives. http://www.washingtondigital archives.org.

Richardson, H. Edward. *Cassius Marcellus Clay: Firebrand of Freedom.* Lexington: University Press of Kentucky, 1976.

Roundtree, Alton G. *The National Grand Lodge and Prince Hall Freemasonry: The Untold Truth.* N.p.: KLD Publishing, LLC.

Rowland, Ira Berlin, and Leslie S. Rowland, eds. *Families & Freedom: A Documentary History of African-American Kinship in the Civil War Era.* New York: New Press, 1997.

Samito, Christian G. *Becoming American Under Fire.* Ithaca, New York: Cornell University Press, 2009.

San Francisco Bulletin. "How the Bowhead Was Crushed." October 4, 1884, 4.

———. "Perils of the Artic: Reported Loss of the Whaling Bark Mabel—Official Investigation into the Loss of the Bowhead—The Catch of the Whaling Fleet." October 27, 1884, 2.

San Francisco Call. "Of Interest to People of the Pacific Coast: Changes Made in the Postal Service and More New Pensions Granted." April 1902, 2.

San Francisco Examiner. "The 'Bowhead' Loss." October 28, 1884, 3.

Schneller, Robert J., Jr. *Cushing: Civil War SEAL.* Dulles, VA: Brassey Incorporated, 2004.

Schubert, Frank N. *Voices of the Buffalo Soldier.* Albuquerque: University of New Mexico Press, 2003.

Schwarzen, Christopher. "Marilyn Quincy Put Work First for 36 Years." *Seattle Times*, March 14, 2007.

Seattle Daily Times. "City Pays Tribute to Lincoln Tonight: Banquet to Be Held in Civic Auditorium, Ex-Slave Pays Tribute." February 12, 1930, 1 and 3.

———. "Coyote Captured on Westlake Avenue." September 13–14, 1921, 3, 13.

———. "Deaths and Funerals." July 8, 1905, 4.

———. "Gideon S. Bailey Dead: Prominent Colored Citizen Passes Away After Long Illness." July 3, 1905, 4.

———. "Heart Attack Kills Woman on Way Home." June 3, 1930, 3.

———. "Henry Carper Get His Share; Retires, Shrewd Real Estate Dealer Says He Believes in Looking After Coming Generation—Came to Sound in 1903." 1910, 2.

———. "Henry Carper Gets His Share; Retires." August 13, 1904.

———. "Master Burglar Stole for Drugs, Says His Father." 1919.

———. "Minister Will Tell Story of Passion Play." April 9, 1910, 7.

———. "Obituary—Anna Bennett." June 6, 1930, 43.

———. "Obituary—Charles Morgan." May 1903, 37.

———. "Obituary—David Clark." October 21, 1921, 13.

———. "Obituary—Edward Clark." August 16, 1932, 17.

———. "Obituary—Green Fields." August 4, 1914, 9.

———. "Obituary—Spencer Jackson." November 20, 1916, 13.

———. "Old Soldiers to Teach Patriotism…." May 21, 1916, 22.

———. "Once Sold on Slave Block, He Pays Homage to Lincoln." February 12, 1930, 1.

———. "Orting Special Correspondence—Charles A. Morgan." May 10, 1903, 37.

———. "Turn in False Fire Alarm." October 16, 1905, 7.

Seattle Daily Times Evening Edition. "Rudolph B. Scott Removed—Secretary Metcalf Dismisses Immigration Agent at Anacortes for Official Delinquencies." February 15, 1906, 9.

Seattle Post-Intelligencer. "Ancient York Masons Organize." May 22, 1892, 16.

———. "Constable Smalley's Luck." May 2, 1894, 5.

———. "Engineer Martin Must Be Tried." November 18, 1894, 8.

———. "Four Lives Are Lost: Another Fatal Fire in Franklin Coal Mine." October 18, 1895, 5.

———. "The Franklin Mine Damage Suit." April 27, 1895, 5.

———. "The Franklin Vote." January 4, 1895, 5.

———. "Grand Barbecue at Newcastle." August 5, 1894, 5.

———. "Grand Lodge of Masons." June 13, 1899, 5.

———. "Joe Bennett a Bad Boy." March 24, 1900, 6.

———. "Judge G.S. Bailey Dead." July 6, 1905, 11.

———. "Noonday Ward Meeting." October 28, 1896, 8.

———. "Obituary—Hervey." September 10, 1920, 14.

———. "Obituary—Hervey." September 12, 1920, 4.

———. "Obituary—Samuel F. Johnson." 1912, 4.

———. "Obituary—Samuel Johnson." May 9 and 10, 1912, 4.

———. "Program Links Civil War and Local History, Snohomish Residents Collection Information on Vets Buried There." April 8, 2002.

———. "Released in Habeas Corpus." May 3, 1894, 5.

———. "Scott vs. Canadian Pacific Railway Company—January 26." January 14, 1894, 5.

———. "They Died Despite Warnings." October 27, 1895, 2.

———. "To Aid the Cubans: Colored Citizens to Hold a Mass Meeting Tonight." May 6, 1896, 8.

———. "Use of Drugs Is Cause of Crimes." 1919.

———. "Washington Pensions—Rudolph B. Scott." October 9, 1896, 2.

———. "Washington Pensions—Rudolph B. Scott Rejected." October 30, 1895, 2.

———. "Where Now Is Todd?" August 12, 1895, 3.

Seattle Republican. "Afro-Americanism." August 10, 1904, 3.

———. "Alfred Hawkins." November 3, 1905, 6.

———. "Appointment of R.B. Scott." February 16, 1906, 21.

———. "Baptist Convention." August 3, 1906, 6.

———. "Brothers in Black." July 11, 1902, 1.

———. "Colored Colonists." November 3, 1905, 6.

———. "Editor Gideon Bailey." October 5, 1900, 1.

———. "Funeral of the Late Judge Gideon S. Bailey." July 7 and 14, 1905, 6 and 8.

———. "Green Fields." From the *Northwest Negro Progress Number, Alaska-Yukon-Pacific Exposition* special edition, 1909, 18.

———. "Joseph Benett." October 4, 1907, 4.

———. "Judge Dead." July 14, 1905, 8.

———. "Judge G.S. Bailey Dead." July 7, 1905.

———. "Mr. Charles S. Barrow—Printer." October 3, 1902, 4.

———. "Mr. Haller Takes Care." October 4, 1907, 4.

———. "Mrs. Minnie Bryan." June 9, 1905, 6.

———. "Mystic Shrine Set Up." July 12, 1902, 4.

———. "The Northwest Negro Progress." June 21, 1907, 5.

———. "Personal." June 3, 1904, 8.

———. "Personal—Donaldson." October 23, 1903, 8.

———. "Personals—Donaldson." April 1, 1904, 8.

———. "A Prominent Afro-American Dies—R. B. Scott." April 2, 1909, 5.

———. "Republican Politicians." February 23, 1900, 3.

———. "Rev. Barrows Injured." August 3, 1906, 6.

———. "Roslyn Notes—Donaldson." December 5, 1902, 4.

———. "Roslyn Notes—Donaldson." October 14, 1904, 7.

———. "Rudolph B. Scott Removed." February 16, 1906, 4.

———. "Summons for Publication—Superior Court—Wiley v. Donaldson, et al." January 21, 1910, 2.

———. "Sunnyside, Washington, February 20, 1905." February 24, 1905, 8.

———. "Sunnyside Scenes." January 27, 1905, 7.

———. "Sunny-Side Scenes." September 27, 1907, 3.

———. "Sunnyside Scribbles." June 17, 1904, 10.

———. "Sunnyside Squibbles." August 5, 1904, 10.

Seattle Republican. October 4, 1902, 3.

Seattle Star. "Aged Father Bares Tragic Secret as Warning Against 'Drug' Habit." 1919.

———. "The Funeral of Clark Harris." July 24, 1911, 8.

———. "Obituary—Clark Harris." July 24, 1911, 8.

Seattle Times. "Digest: Threats Increase in Highway 99 Debate." 2002.

Semi-Weekly Knoxville Sentinel. April 4, 1894, 4.

Smith, John David. *Black Soldiers in Blue: African American Troops in the Civil War Era.* Chapel Hill: University of North Carolina, 2002.

Snohomish County Tribune. "Obituary—William Stewart." December 11, 1907.

———. "Possibly a Tragedy—Riderless Horse Found with Turned Saddle." December 29, 1899.

Speer, Lonnie R. *Portals to Hell: Military Prisons of the Civil War.* Mechanicsburg, PA: Stackpole Books, 1997.

Spokane Daily Chronicle. "The Blacks Helped Build City in Many Way." February 7, 1985, 23.

———. "Colonel Atkins Dead." August 6, 1897, 7.

———. "Death of R.B. Scott." March 23, 1909, 3.

———. "Deaths—Walter Scott." January 6, 1923, 14.

———. "Early Blacks Trove Here." November 26, 1981, 28.

———. "Family History: Black Pioneer Sought a Living." February 19, 1979, 3.

———. "Funeral Colonel Atkins." August 7, 1897, 5.

———. "Noble Life of Rev. Barrow." July 30, 1906, 11.

———. "Obituary—Charles James." October 28, 1925, 6.

———. "Obituary—Walter Scott." January 8, 1923, 17.

Spokane Press. "Big Fruit Farm." June 27, 1904, 1.

———. "Burn Mortgage." February 26, 1906, 2.

———. "Chinaman May Be Deported." May 21, 1904, 1.

———. "Chinese Funeral Is Delayed by Red Tape." February 10, 1905, 1.

———. "Four Chinamen Arrested." July 7, 1904, 1.

———. "Harris Wants Investigation." April 8, 1909, 1.

———. "Injury Proves Fatal." July 30, 1906, 4.

———. "Officer Elected." December 21, 1904, 4.

———. "Preacher's Son Goes to Prison." July 15, 1904, 1.

———. "Settle Minister's Death for $150." November 1, 1906, 1.

———. "Were Deported: Five Chinamen Sent Back to the Orient." November 15, 1902, 1.

Spokesman-Review. "Calvary Baptist Church." November 8, 2013, 1.

———. "Mrs. Scott's Funeral Friday." June 5, 1924, 5.

———. "Pioneer of City Dies of Injuries." July 30, 1906, 10.

———. "Rev. P.B. Barrows' Funeral." August 1, 1906, 7.

Spurgeon, Ian Michael. *Soldiers in the Army of Freedom: The 1ˢᵗ Kansas Colored, the Civil War's First African American Combat Unit.* Norman: University of Oklahoma Press, 2014.

Squire, William. "The 24ᵗʰ Infantry Regiment and the Racial Debate in the U.S. Army." Master's thesis, U.S. Army Command and General Staff College, University of Tennessee, 1985.

St. Louis Palladium. "City News." October 29, 1904, 8.

St. Paul Daily Globe. "At Society Hall." January 5, 1890, 10.

———. "Blanket Thief—Clark Harris." March 20, 1890, 8.

———. "Charge with Bigamy—Clark Harris." December 3, 1892, 2.

———. "Court Brief—Clark Harris." December 11, 1892, 6.

———. "Minneapolis Globules." October 19, 1889, 3.

———. "Newsboys' Club Rooms Moved." March 20, 1892, 11.

———. "Salvation Army Morals." January 30, 1892, 2.

———. "Thief Sentenced." March 22, 1890, 2.

St. Paul Daily Press. "Police Court—Clark Harris, Disorderly Behavior." August 8, 1869.

St. Paul Globe. "Clark Harris Free: The Alleged Bigamist Discharged by Judge Otis." December 13, 1892, 2.

———. "Thief of Blanket from Clark Harris." March 21, 1890, 2.

Sunnyside Sun. "Aged Negro Drops Dead." October 2, 1913, 5.

———. "Court Decides Mortgage Was a Forged One." September 25, 1913, 1.

Sutherland, Johnathan. *African Americans at War: An Encyclopedia.* Knoxville, TN: ABC-CLIO, 2003.

Tacoma Daily Ledger. "G.A.R. Attention—Files." August 2, 1914. Newspaper.com.

———. "Local Death Record (Barrow)." July 30, 1906, 5.

Tacoma Daily News. "Coroner's Verdict." August 27, 1894, 1.

———. "Injury Alone Not Fatal." July 30, 1906, 3.

———. "30 Persons Are Hurled from Cable Car." July 24, 1906, 2.

Tacoma News Tribune. "Obituary—Nicholas Johnson." July 5, 1934, 4.

Taylor, Quintard. *In Search of the Racial Frontier: African Americans in the American West, 1528–1990.* New York: W.W. Norton & Company, 1998.

Taylor, Susie King. *Reminiscences of Life in Camp with the 33ʳᵈ United States Colored Troops Late 1ˢᵗ S.C. Volunteers.* Boston, MA: self-published, 1902.

Trudeau, Noah Andre. *Like Men of War: Black Troops in the Civil War, 1862–1865.* Edison, NJ: Castle Books, 1998.

The Union Army: Cyclopedia of Battles. Volume 6, *A History of Military Affairs in the Loyal States 1861–65—Records of the Regiments in the Army.* Madison, WI: Federal Publishing Company, 1908.

"U.S. City Directories, 1821–1989." Portland, Oregon. http://www.ancestry.com.

U.S. Customs Services, Records of the U.S. Coast Guard. Shipping Articles and Crew Lists, 1851–1950.

U.S. Public Health Service. "Clinical Record, History of Present Disease, Joseph P. Bennett." July 8, 1935.

U.S. Public Health Service, Marine Hospital. "Autopsy Report Joseph Bennett." July 10, 1935.

"United States Veterans Administration Pension Payment Cards, 1907–1933, Index and Images." NARA Microfilm Publication M850. National Archives and Records Administration. Family Search. https://familysearch.org.

Urwin, Gregory J.L., ed. *Black Flag Over Dixie: Racial Atrocities and Reprisals in the Civil War*. Carbondale: Southern Illinois University, 2004.

Verhovek, Sam Howe. "Road Named for Jeffeson Davis Stirs Spirited Debate." *New York Times*, February 14, 2002.

Ward, Andrew. *The Battle of Plum Run and the Civil War on the Mississippi*. Davis, CA: Back Burner Press, 2010.

Warren, Lillian C., and Robert E. Williams. *The Donaldson Odyssey: Footsteps to Freedom*. Seattle, WA: Lillian Warren, 1991.

Washington, Kittitas County. Wills and Probate Records, 1807–1997. Ancestry.com.

Washington, Versalle F. *Eagles on Their Buttons*. Columbia: University of Missouri Press, 1999.

Washington Standard. "Washington Pensions Granted." April 18, 1902, 1.

Washington State Digital Archives. "Washington State Penitentiary, Commitment Registers and Mug Shots, 1887–1946."

Weekly Clarion (Jackson, MS). "Local Legislature." November 10, 1870, 1.

———. "The Radicals in Warren County." December 9, 1869, 2.

———. "The Radicals in Warren County." October 20, 1875, 3.

Welch, Jack. "Hot Work: The Northern Pacific Coal Company Brings African American Strikebreakers to Roslyn." *Columbia: The Magazine of Northwest History* (Winter 2013–14): 5–10.

Weldman, Budge. "The Fight for Equal Rights—Black Soldiers in the Civil War." Teaching with Documents, 1997. http://www.archives.gov/education/lessons/blacks-civil-war/article.html.

Western Appeal (St. Paul, MN). "Locals." March 19, 1887, 1.

Wikipedia. "Nicholas M. Nolan." https://en.wikipedia.org/wiki/Nicholas_M._Nolan.

Williams, Greg H. *Civil War Suits in the U.S. Court of Claims: Cases Involving Compensaion to Northerners and Southerners for Wartime Losses*. Jefferson, NC: MacFarland and Company Inc., Publishers, 2006.

Williams, Janet. "Civil War Marker Sparks New Conflict." BBC News, May 6, 2002.

Wilson, Cynthia, and Donna Kennedy. "Press Article Brings More Civil War Vet Facts to Light." *Issaquah Press*, February 25, 2009, A6.

Wilson, Joseph T. *The Black Phalanx: African American Soldiers in the War of Independence, the War of 1812 and the Civil War*. Hartford, CT: American Publishing Company, 1890.

Wright, E.W. *Marine History of the Pacific Northwest*. Seattle, WA: Superior Publishing Company, 1967.

Wyeth, John Allan. *The Life of General Nathan Bedford Forrest*. United States: Barnes & Noble Publishing Inc., 2006.

Wyllie, Arthur. *The Union Navy*. United States: Lulu Printing, 2007.

Yakima Daily Republic. "Frenzied Finance in Superior Court Case." September 24, 1913.

———. "Negro Soldier Is Killed by Joy." September 25, 1913, 1.

———. "Obituary—Hawkins." September 25, 1913, 1.

Yakima Herald. "City News in Brief." March 1, 1905, 10.

———. "Colony Is Planned." April 14, 1909.

———. "Colored Men for the Right." December 1, 1909, 7.

———. "Encampment of the G.A.R. at Ellensburg." June 21, 1900, 5.

———. "Hops." January 4, 1905, 10.

———. "Hops." March 1, 1905, 10.

———. "Notice of Real Estate Sale." October 16, 1907, 3.

———. "Notice of Real Estate Sale." October 9, 1907, 5.

———. "Notice of Sheriff's Sale of Real Estate." October 2, 1907, 5.

———. "Plundered a Merchant." March 29, 1900, 1.

———. "Sunnyside." March 15, 1900, 10.

———. "Sunnyside." March 21, 1906, 10.

———. "Throughout the County." March 15, 1900, 10.

———. "Well Drilling Plants at Work in the Selah: Homestead Says He Saw Six at Work in a Drive Twenty Miles to the City," 1910.

Yakima Morning Herald. "Aged Negro Drops Dead—A.A. Hawkins." September 26, 1913, 1.

———. "Land Restored to Aged Negro." September 24, 1913, 1.

Yakima Valley Memories: The Early Years. Canada: Pediment Publishing, 2004.

Young, Miriam, and Donna Bogumill, eds. *A Comprehensive History of the Washington Soldiers' Home and Colony, 1891–1991: 100 Years of Service to Our State's Veterans.* N.p.: Washington Veterans Home, 1991.

Affidavits from Pension Files

General Affidavit, Bailey, Mary E. Seattle, King County, Washington, August 1907.

General Affidavit, Bailey, Mary E. Seattle, King County, Washington, July 1906.

General Affidavit, Donaldson, Jessee. Hamilton County, Tennessee, April 24, 1893.

General Affidavit, Donaldson, Jessee. Hamilton County, Tennessee, July 21, 1892.

General Affidavit, Donaldson, Jessee. Roslyn, Kittitas County, Washington, June 13, 1901.

General Affidavit, Evans, Belle, for Augustus Dixon. State of Washington, County of Yakima, May 19, 1903.

General Affidavit, Hawkins, Alfred Allin. Yakima County, Washington, 1898.

General Affidavit, Phillips, William C., for Augustus Dixon. State of Washington, County of Pierce, May 19, 1908.

Deposition of/for Claimant

Barrow, Peter B. April 22, 1895.

Dale, Edna V., MD, for Jasper Evans, September 21, 1926.

Dixon, Augustus. Guthrie, Logan County, Oklahoma Territory, July 2, 1887.

Donaldson, Jessee. Marion County, Tennessee, June 7, 1889.

Evans, Jasper, to Pension Board, December 27, 1901.

Hollins, Columbus, to the State of Washington, County of Pierce, May 26, 1914.

Hunter, Arta. Boonville, Warrick County, Indiana, August 11, 1901.

Plummer, Newton B. Belknap, New Hampshire, September 4, 1903.

Smith, Mary J. For Henry Carper, Knoxville, Tennessee, October 17, 1921.

Spencer, Bryant. Identified his brother as John in a deposition dated October 9, 1885.

Letters

Ainsworth, T.C., Colonel, U.S. Army, Chief, Record and Pension Offices, to "Sir" Messer's A. Legg & Company, Attorneys, Washington, D.C., March 2, 1894.

Black, Andrew R., to "Gentlemen," Department of the Interior, August 12, 1911.

Black, Andrew R., to "Gentlemen," Department of the Interior, August 30, 1911.

Black, Andrew R., to "Gentlemen," Department of the Interior, May 12, 1912.

Black, Andrew R., to "Gentlemen," Department of the Interior, November 24, 1911.

Black, John C., to "Dear Sir" Bureau of Pensions, November 26, 1888.

Brown, Paul B. Textual Reference Operations, National Archives at College Park, Maryland, to "Dear Ms. Wilson," May 11, 2022.

Chief of Law Division to "Sir" Chief of the S.E. Division of Bureau of Pensions, December 2, 1903.

Donegan, Julie, "Dear Sir" Commissioner of Pension, December 17, 1925.

Expenses of U.S. v. Jessee Donaldson, to Edwin C. Miller Warden from R.M. Hopkins, Clerk, March 3, 1903.

Haswell, George, Special Examiner, to "Sir" Commissioner of Pensions, September 30, 1884. Report of James Abell.

Hervey, Carey, to "Dear Sir," Commissioner of Pension, date unknown.

Hervey, Carey, to "Dear Sir," Department of Interior, September 5, 1922.

Larkins, Samuel, to "Gentlemen," Hon Board of Control, Olympia, Washington, October 25, 1907.

Scott, Mrs. Alice M., to "Dear Sir" Washington Gardner, Commissioner of Pensions, October 8, 1924.

Smith, John A., Esq., Clerk Circuit Court, D.C., May 20, 1862, signed by Barbara Williams, Washington, D.C. Slave Emancipation Records, 1851–63. Report of Henry Carper.

Stillwell, L., Acting Commission, to "Sir" Andrew R. Black, September 6, 1912.

Taylor, Guy, Disbursing Clerk, to "Dear Chief, Finance Division of the Pension Office," and to "Dear Carey Hervey," October 28, 1920.

Surgeon's Certificates

Clark, David. Gray's Lake, Idaho, January 20, 1895.

Evans, Jasper. Claim no. 580022. Yakima, Yakima County, Washington.

Henson, Frank. Ellensburg, Kittitas County, Washington, November 23, 1904.

Index

ABOUT THE AUTHOR

Cynthia Wilson is an independent researcher of African American military men of the mid-eighteenth to early nineteenth centuries. Formerly member of the board of directors of the Black Heritage Society of Washington State Inc., she also headed the Black Genealogy Research Group (BGRG) for four years. She contributed several short stories of notable individuals to Quintard Taylor's website BlackPast (blackpast.org).

Visit us at
www.historypress.com